THE
RHYTHMS
OF
JEWISH
LIVING

THE RHYTHMS OF JEWISH LIVING

A Sephardic Exploration of the
Basic Teachings of Judaism

MARC D. ANGEL

𝒜

JASON ARONSON INC.
Northvale, New Jersey
Jerusalem

This book was set in 11 pt. Melior by Alabama Book Composition of Deatsville, AL.

10   9   8   7   6   5   4   3   2

Library of Congress Cataloging-in-Publication Data

Angel, Marc.
    The rhythms of Jewish living : a Sephardic exploration of the
basic teachings of Judaism / by Marc D. Angel.
        p.   cm.
    Previously published: New York : Sepher–Hermon Press, 1986.
    Includes bibliographical references and index.
    ISBN 0–7657–9983–9
    1. Judaism—Essence, genius, nature. 2. Sephardim. I. Title.
BM565.A73 1997
296.7—dc21   97–25576
                                              CIP

Manufactured in the United States of America. Jason Aronson Inc. offers books and cassettes. For information and catalog write to Jason Aronson Inc., 230 Livingston Street, Northvale, New Jersey 07647.

For Gilda,
for every reason

CONTENTS

INTRODUCTION

A Midrash teaches that the way of Torah is a narrow path. On the right is fire and on the left is ice. If one veers from the path, one will be destroyed by either the fire or the ice.

The Torah way of life is balanced, harmonious, and sensible. It imbues life with depth, meaning, and true happiness.

Yet, it has not always been easy for people to stay on the path.

Veering to the left freezes the soul of Judaism. Classic Judaism expresses itself through the Bible, Jewish law, and rabbinic teachings. These are the source of its warmth and harmony. They imbue the rhythms of Jewish living. When one abandons Jewish belief and observance, this is a turn towards the ice. Inevitably, this leads to a breakdown in Jewish experience and Jewish identity.

In veering to the right of the path of Torah, one faces the spiritual destruction of fire—excessive zeal, religious extremism. This tendency manifests itself in a spirit of isolationism, self-righteousness, and xenophobia. It reduces the Torah way of life to self-imposed physical and spiritual ghettos.

This book seeks to present a viable framework for a balanced and harmonious understanding of Judaism's way of life. It steers a course which avoids the ice on the left and the fire on the right.

My hope is that this book will open a new window of understanding of Judaism for its readers. If so, my labor is well rewarded.

Marc D. Angel

ACKNOWLEDGMENTS

This book emerged from a series of courses I gave for Congregation Shearith Israel and Sephardic House. An underlying concern of the classes was to deal with the basic patterns of Jewish living and to explore their meaning for modern Jews.

I thank all those who attended the original classes and who participated in the discussions. I learned much from them. I thank Mrs. Hennie Imberman for her technical assistance in preparing the manuscript and for her general helpfulness.

The first edition of this book was published by Sefer-Hermon Press for Sephardic House. I thank the staff of Jason Aronson Inc. for their wonderful cooperation in producing this edition of the book.

A special word of thanks goes to my son, Rabbi Hayyim Angel, whose various suggestions have been incorporated into this new edition.

My wife, Gilda, was of inestimable assistance in all phases of the development of this book. Her many profound and sensitive insights are reflected throughout the work. I thank her and our children, Hayyim, Ronda and Dan Arking, and Elana and James Nussbaum.

1. THE RHYTHMS OF NATURE

Creation

To a religious person, the universe is filled with hidden voices and secret meanings. The natural world, being the creation of God, signals the awesomeness of its Creator.

The Torah opens with the dramatic words: "In the beginning, God created the heavens and the earth." It does not begin with the story of God's revelation to the Israelites at Sinai; nor with specific commandments. The first chapter of Genesis establishes in powerful terms that God created the universe and everything within it.

An ancient Aramaic translation of the Torah interprets the Hebrew word "bereishith" (in the beginning) to mean "behokhmah" (with wisdom).[1] According to this translation, the Torah opens with the statement: "With wisdom did God create the heavens and the earth." A human being, by recognizing the vast wisdom of God as reflected in the universe He created, comes to a profound awareness of his relationship with God. Indeed, experiencing God as Creator is the beginning of religious wisdom.

Moses Maimonides, the pre-eminent Jewish thinker of the middle ages, has understood this truth. He wrote:

Now what is the way that leads to the love of Him and the reverence for Him? When a person contemplates His great and wondrous acts and creations, obtaining from them a

1

glimpse of His wisdom, which is beyond compare and infinite, he will promptly love and glorify Him, longing exceedingly to know the great Name of God, as David said: 'My
whole being thirsts for God, the living God (Psalm 42:3)'.
When he ponders over these very subjects, he will immediately recoil, startled, conceiving that he is a lowly, obscure
creature . . . as David said: 'As I look up to the heavens Your
fingers made . . . what is man that you should think of him
(Psalm 8:4-5)?[2]

The source of the love and fear of God rests in the contemplation of the world which God created.

The Torah and the Natural Universe

By opening with the story of creation, the Torah teaches
that one must have a living relationship with the natural
world in order to enter and maintain a living relationship
with God. Jewish spirituality flowers and deepens through
this relationship. The ancient sacred texts of Judaism, beginning with the Torah itself, guide us to live with a keen
awareness of the rhythms of nature.

Jewish spirituality is organically linked to the natural
rhythms of the universe. To a great extent, Jewish religious
traditions serve to bring Jews into a sensitive relationship
with the natural world. Many commandments and customs
lead Jews in this direction, drawing out the love and reverence which emerge from the contemplation of God's creations.

An ancient teaching is that God "looked into the Torah
and created the world."[3] This statement reflects a belief that
the Torah actually predated Creation, and served as the
blueprint for the universe. This enigmatic teaching has been
subject to various interpretations. But perhaps its main intent
is to reveal the organic connection between the Torah and the
universe. Since the laws of the Torah are linked to nature, it is
as though nature was created to fit these laws. The natural
world was created in harmony with the revealed words of the

Torah. A Talmudic statement teaches that God created the world only on condition that Israel would accept the Torah. If not, the world would again be reduced to chaos and void.[4]

The Talmud (Makkot 23b) teaches that God gave the people of Israel 613 commandments. There are 248 positive commandments, corresponding to the number of limbs in the human body. And there are 365 negative commandments, corresponding to the number of days in the solar year. This means that the Torah's commandments are ingrained in our very being; in our limbs, in the years of our lives. God's original design in Creation was related to His original design of the Torah and its commandments. The natural universe and the spiritual universe are in rhythm with each other.

This harmony may also be implicit in the blessing recited after reading from the Torah. The blessing extols God "Who has given us His Torah, the Torah of truth, and has planted within us eternal life (hayyei olam)." The phrase hayyei olam has been understood to refer to the eternal soul of each person; or to the Torah which is the source of eternal life for the people of Israel. Yet, perhaps the blessing also suggests another dimension of meaning.

The world olam in Biblical Hebrew usually refers to time—a long duration, eternity. In later Hebrew, olam came to mean "the world," referring to space rather than specifically to time. Hayyei olam, therefore, may be understood as "eternal life," but also as "the life of the world". The blessing may be echoing both meanings. Aside from relating to eternal life, the blessing might be understood as praising God for planting within us the life of the world. That is, through His Torah, God has tied our lives to the rhythms of the natural world. Through this connection with the natural world, we are brought into a living relationship with God.

Jewish tradition, thus, has two roads to God: the natural world, which reveals God as Creator; and the Torah, which records the words of God to the people of Israel. But the Torah itself leads us back to the first road, the road of experiencing

God as Creator. The Torah and nature are bound together.

The relationship of Torah and nature is evident in Psalm 19. This psalm has played an important role in Jewish religious consciousness, since it is included in the Sabbath liturgy—and is read daily in some communities. The psalm has two distinct parts, which at first glance seem to be unconnected. It begins: "The heavens declare the glory of God, and the firmament tells His handiwork. Day unto day utters the tale, night unto night unfolds knowledge. There is no word, no speech, their voice is not heard, yet their course extends through all the world, and their theme to the end of the world." It goes on to describe the sun which rejoices as a strong man prepared to run his course. "Its setting forth is from one end of the skies, its circuit unto the other extreme, and nothing is hidden from its heat." Then the psalm makes an abrupt shift. It continues: "The law of the Lord is perfect, comforting the soul . . . the precepts of the Lord are right, rejoicing the heart. The commandment of the Lord is clear, enlightening the eyes." From a description of the glory of God as manifested in the natural world, the psalm jumps to a praise of the Torah, God's special revelation to the people of Israel. The psalm seems to be composed of two separate segments, as if accidentally put together by a careless editor.

But the psalm, in its present form, has been part of the Jewish religious tradition for thousands of years. Its impact on Jews has been as a unitary literary piece.

The enigma of this psalm's organization, however, is easily solved. Psalm 19 is teaching that one may come to an understanding of God both through the natural world and through the Torah. God has given us two roads to Him.

This concept underlies the organization of Jewish prayers, both for the morning and evening services. In both of these services, the recitation of the *Shema*—the Biblical passage proclaiming the unity of God—is a central feature. In each service, the *Shema* is introduced by two sections, each concluding with a blessing. Although the words of these sections vary between the two services, their themes are the same. The first section praises God as Creator, the One Who called the universe into being, Who set the sun, moon and stars in their rhythms, Who separated between day and night. The second section praises God as the giver of the Torah, as the One Who loves Israel. Only after reciting both sections do we recite the Shema and the subsequent prayers. The God of creation and the God of revelation are One, and we may find our way to Him through His world of creation and through His revealed word.

Sunrise

Certain moments in the day are particularly conducive to pensiveness. At dawn, with the rising of the sun, the sky in the east awakens with color and light. At sunrise, one experiences the still-fading darkness of night along with the faintly emerging light of day. It is an in-between time, vague, pregnant with possibility.

Jewish tradition has long taught that the ideal time for morning prayer is at sunrise. It is considered particularly virtuous to pray at that time, when the prayer is in harmony with the emerging sun. The prayer of the morning extols God, Who "in His goodness ever revives each day anew His work of creation." The rising sun is symbolic of this daily re-creation of the universe. At the very moment when the sun rises and the world seems to be re-created—that is the preferred moment for the morning prayer. In that mysterious, quiet, in-between time, we experience God the Creator both in the skies and in the words of our prayerbook.

Sunset

Sundown, too, is a mysterious and poetic time. The sun is dropping out of sight. The sky in the west is streaked with red and purple. In a short while, the world will be plunged into darkness.

Again, Jewish tradition has understood the connection

of human spirituality with the natural world. Jewish law prescribes that the afternoon prayers be recited before the sun sets. Many Jews recite the afternoon prayers just as the sun is setting. The night prayers are to be said ideally when the stars in the sky can be seen.

The daily prayer rhythm brings the worshipper into the natural rhythm of sunrise and sunset.

Midnight

The power of night, especially before the development of electric lights, was enormous. Without streetlights and other artificial lighting, the darkness of night is awesome, frightening. The cycle of light and darkness profoundly affected the lives of almost everyone. During the day, people would be able to be outdoors, to work, tend the farm, visit friends and neighbors. But at night, the fear of darkness took hold. People preferred to remain in their homes, in their enclosed world of relative safety.

The darkness of night, in spite of the fear it can engender, also presents a remarkable unfolding of God's creation: the stars. A person may enhance his spiritual life by going outside at night and gazing at the stars. This experience will cause him to fall into a state of awe and wonder. He will appreciate the greatness of God and feel the elevation of his own soul.

Midnight, as the furthest point into the darkness, is a particularly haunting time.

Kabbalists connected their spirituality to midnight. Rabbi Abraham Halevy, of 16th century Safed, reported that the pious Jews of his town would awaken each night in order to recite a special set of prayers—at midnight. They sat on the ground, wrapped in black, and lamented the destruction of the ancient Temple in Jerusalem.[5] At midnight, the darkest moment in the daily cycle, the mystics cried and prayed over the darkest moment in the spiritual life of the Jewish people. But the lamentations, with all their sadness, were also imbued with hope. After all, midnight was the furthest one could fall into darkness. From then on, the movement was toward sunrise, toward redemption. The mystics associated the experiences of the Jewish people with the cycle of the sun. To this day, the midnight vigil—known as *Tikkun Hatsot*—is observed among pious Jews.

The Moon

The religious mind has alway been intrigued by the heavens above. Religious language speaks of "our God in heaven," "our Father in heaven." Heaven may be understood allegorically i.e. God is transcendent, beyond reach. The fact that religious imagery places God in heaven reflects a deep religious sentiment that God is experienced by our musings about heaven. Humans entertain thoughts of God's transcendence upon contemplating the sun, stars and moon of the heavens.

While the daily cycle is governed by sunrise and sunset, the monthly cycle is the domain of the moon. Mircea Eliade, the noted religious anthropologist, has observed that "it is through the moon's phases—that is, its birth, death, and resurrection—that men came to know at once their own mode of being in the cosmos and the chances for their survival or rebirth."[6] Lunar symbolism has had a profound place in religious thought. Eliade suggests that it enabled people to connect such heterogeneous things as birth, becoming, death, resurrection; the waters, plants, woman, fecundity, immortality; cosmic darkness, pre-natal existence, life after death, rebirth; fate, temporality, death; and others. The moon is symbolic of human life. Its rhythmical cycles keep it ever changing. It has a dark, unknown side. And even its light is muted and mysterious.

Professor Gershom Scholem has commented on the role of the moon in kabbalistic thought. "No cosmic event seemed to the kabbalists to be more closely connected with the exile of all things, with the imperfection and the taint inherent in all being, than this periodic lessening of the moon."[7] Scholem points out the striking convergence of two themes which were to dominate the kabbalah from the 16th century on: the catastrophe of exile, and the regeneration of the light after its total disappearance. The moon, in its waning, symbolized the exile into darkness. But the same moon, in its rebirth, symbolized the promise that all things would one day be rectified through redemption.

In ancient Israel, the day of the new moon (*Rosh Hodesh*) was celebrated as a joyous festival. When the great rabbinical court functioned in Jerusalem during the days of the Temple, witnesses who sighted the beginnings of the moon would come to court and testify concerning their sighting. The court would then declare that the new month had begun. A celebration was held in honor of all those who came to testify.

The Jewish festivals and holy days were determined by the court's declaration of the new moon, based on the testimony of reliable witnesses. Thus, Israelites would search the heavens for the sign of the emerging moon, since the moon was so important to their religious calendar. *Rosh Hodesh* has continued to be observed as a minor festival throughout the centuries, including our own day.

The mystics of 16th century Safed attached great significance to *Rosh Hodesh*. They also observed the day preceding the new moon as a fast day, devoted to meditation on the themes of exile and redemption. This day became known as *Yom Kippur Kattan*, the minor Day of Atonement.

One of the mystics, Rabbi Abraham Galante, listed rules for the pious people to follow.[8] Among them, he described the practices observed on the day prior to the new moon. Everyone fasted — men, women and young students. They gathered in one place and remained there all day reciting penitential prayers, confessions, and also giving each other lashes. Some people placed a large rock on their stomachs, symbolic of the fact that they considered themselves guilty of crimes punishable by stoning; some choked themselves with their hands. Some climbed into a sack and had someone drag them around the synagogue. On the eve of the new moon, some had the custom of arising at midnight to read from the book of Psalms. These observances, though tending to be ascetic, demonstrated the connection between the spirituality of the people and the rhythm of the moon. The moon itself became a feature of their religious life.

A widely observed custom to this day is the recitation of a special blessing upon witnessing the moon in its brightness and its fullness. The proper time for this blessing is on a night between the seventh and fifteenth days of the lunar cycle. In many communities, it has been customary to recite this blessing on a Saturday night, after the conclusion of the Shabbat. At that time people are still dressed in their Shabbat clothes and are still imbued with the joy of Shabbat. The blessing over the moon is to be recited on a clear night when the moon is visible, not hidden behind clouds.

The Talmud (Sanhedrin 42a) reports the opinion of Rabbi Aha bar Hanina who stated in the name of Rabbi Asi who stated in the name of Rabbi Yohanan: "One who blesses the new moon at the proper time is as one who has received the Divine Presence." Rabbi David Abudarham, the medieval Spanish-Jewish commentator on the prayer book, explained this Talmudic passage as follows: even though God is not seen by the human eye, He is seen by means of His marvels and wonders. He reveals Himself to us by means of the renewal of the moon.[9]

The blessing over the moon is generally accompanied by the chanting of certain psalms and Biblical verses. The actual text of the blessing is:

> Blessed are You, Lord our God, King of the universe, Who created the heavens with His word, and with the breath of His mouth all their host. He gave them a decree and a time that they not change their appointed task. They rejoice and are glad to do the will of their Master. He is a true worker Whose

works are truth. And to the moon He said that it should be renewed, a crown of beauty for the ones carried from the womb, who, in the future, will be renewed (like the moon) to thank their Creator because of the glory of His kingdom. Blessed are You God, renewer of the months.

This blessing expresses the recognition that God created the heavenly spheres and set them into an eternal pattern. The moon is described as a crown of beauty for human beings, a symbol of the renewal which people will experience. The moon, in some ways, is a prefiguration of human experience.

The blessing for the new moon is generally recited outdoors, in the presence of a quorum of at least ten men. It is in no way to be considered as moon worship, but rather as the worship of God, inspired by the regularity and the mystery of the moon. The blessing of the moon concludes with a quotation from the Talmud (Sanhedrin 42a): "It was taught in the school of Rabbi Ishmael that if the children of Israel would be received by their Father in heaven only once a month, it would be enough. Said Abbaye, Let us stand in reverence when we thank God for the new moon."

The Seasons

The seasons of the year influence the foods we eat, the clothes we wear, the activities we perform, and even the way we feel. The yearly cycle of seasons passes from the blossoms of the spring, to the heat of the summer, to the colorful decline of autumn, to the cold of winter.

The Biblical festivals occur at the beginning of autumn —Rosh Hashanah, Yom Kippur, Succoth; and at the beginning of spring—Passover. Shabuoth, which is only a one-day festival in Israel and a two-day observance in the Diaspora, occurs seven weeks after the second night of Passover, and is connected to the Passover festival by the counting of the Omer. All of these festivals are linked to the harvests of autumn and spring, natural times for human beings to rejoice and express thanksgiving to God.

There may be an additional spiritual message in the timing of the festivals. Spring is the season of rebirth and promise; autumn is the beginning of decline, and points to future desolation. Summer and winter are the extreme seasons, while spring and autumn are transitional seasons. It is in autumn and spring that we are most aware of the process of nature, when we see the changes before our eyes. And it is in times of transition and change when the power of God is most apparent.

An Autumn Fire Festival

In chapter three, we will discuss the significance of the festivals. Presently, we are concerned with their relationship to the rhythms of the seasons, to the rhythms of nature. In this connection, it is interesting to consider a special celebration held in the ancient Temple in Jerusalem on the night following the first day of Succoth.

Known as "Simhat Bet Hashoevah," many scholars have believed that it was a water festival, involving water libations and prayers to God for an abundance of rainfall during the coming season. Some scholars, however, have suggested that this celebration was actually a fire festival.

The Mishnah (Succah, Chapter 5) describes the Simhat Bet Hashoevah celebration as being tremendously joyous. Our sages have stated that "one who has not seen the joy of Bet Hashoevah has not seen joy in his life." Studying the Mishnah's description of the celebration will shed light on its meaning.

The Mishnah relates that at the conslusion of the first day of the holiday, the people gathered in the women's section of the Temple. Young priests would ascend golden candelabra and fill the cups with oil. The wicks used were made from worn out priestly vestments. When the candelabra were lit, "there was not an alleyway in Jerusalem that was not lit up from the light of Bet Hashoevah." The sages and pious people danced with torches of fire in their hands and sang words of praise to God. The Levites played their harps, lyres, cymbals, trumpets and innumerable musical instruments, while they stood on the fifteen stairs connecting the women's section with the Israelite men's section.

Two priests stood at the upper gate, holding trumpets. The celebration carried through the night, and at the sound of the crowing of the rooster in the early morning, the priests sounded the trumpets. They descended to the tenth step, and again sounded the trumpets. When they reached the women's section, they sounded the trumpets a third time. They continued to sound the trumpets until they reached the gate which exited to the east. Having reached that gate, the people turned to the west and said: "Our ancestors who were in this place turned their backs to the ark of God and faced the east, and they bowed eastward to the sun. But we, our eyes face God." Rabbi Yehudah said: They would say: "We are for God, and to God we lift our eyes."

The historian, Solomon Zeitlin, deduces from the Mishnah that the Israelites during the time of the First Temple used this occasion to bow in an eastward direction towards the rising sun. The Israelites of the Second Temple, though, rejected the custom of their ancestors and specifically turned to the west upon leaving the Temple, keeping their eyes directed to the holy ark, rather than to the sun.[10]

It is clear from the above description that the ceremony of Bet Hashoevah had something to do with the sun. The fire and torches which characterized the celebration were symbolic of the sun. Though the Jews of the Second Temple did not bow to the sun, those of the First Temple did do so. In origin, then, the festival was connected to the sun. Why?

An answer may be derived from the Biblical verse which describes Succoth as "the festival of the ingathering at the turn of the year" (Exodus 34:22). The autumn festival occurs at the "turn of the year," when the hours of daylight are declining with each passing day. Going into the autumn, one could easily foresee the arrival of winter, with its very short days and very long nights. The power of the sun might appear to be in decline. Therefore, at this season of the turn of the year, the Israelites connected their religious celebration to the sun. They filled the night with torches and fire, the sounds of trumpets and music—at the time of the rising sun. They proclaimed their faithfulness to God, Creator of the sun.

Vestiges of the ancient Temple celebration have continued to exist in various Jewish communities, though the original meaning of the holiday is hardly recognized. It has been customary among middle-eastern communities to light many lamps in their synagogues in honor of Simhat Bet Hashoevah, and to let the lights glow throughout the night.

Springtime

In the Jewish calendar, the spring season begins with the month of Nissan. This is the time when trees are beginning to blossom and when the natural world is starting to flower with color and new life.

Jewish tradition prescribes that during the month of Nissan, Jews should visit orchards or gardens so that they may see trees with new blossoms. This visit is to be done in groups, to lend a communal aspect to the celebration. The blessing to be recited upon seeing trees with new blossoms is: "Blessed are You Lord our God King of the universe, Who has not omitted anything from His world, and has created good creatures and good trees to give pleasure to human beings." The blessing is in gratitude for the human pleasure derived from observing the beauties of nature. According to Jewish law, this blessing is to be recited only once each year, as a reminder of the yearly renewal of nature which comes about through the power of God. The blessing is to be recited while the tree is newly blossoming, not when fruit has already grown on it. The blessing is not on the fruit, but on the renewal of nature which God brings each springtime.[11]

The Torah refers to Passover as "the spring festival." It must always occur during the springtime. This rule determines calendar calculations. Months are based on a lunar cycle, each month beginning with the new moon. However, the lunar year has only 354 days, compared to the 365 days of the solar calendar. If the Jews followed only the lunar cycle, Passover would not necessarily occur during the springtime. (The Moslems do follow a lunar calendar and their holidays are not bound to any season.) The Jewish sages of antiquity devised a cycle in which there are seven leap years during each nineteen year cycle. Each leap year has one full month added (Second Adar). Thus, the lunar calendar is brought into harmony with the solar calendar—and Passover always occurs in the springtime.

Tu B'Shvat

The first Mishnah in the Talmudic tractate of Rosh Hashanah refers to the fifteenth day of the month of Shevat (*Tu B'Shvat*) as the new year for trees. This date marked the starting point for tithing fruits in ancient Israel. The significance of the date expanded over the centuries so that this minor holiday has become associated with a celebration of the abundance of nature. The observances of *Tu B'Shvat* were broadened under the influence of Rabbi Hayyim Vital and other 16th century Sephardic kabbalists living in Safed. From Safed, these customs spread throughout Asia, North Africa and Europe.

Tu B'Shvat prayers and readings were arranged in a distinctive order for use in a service. In the mid-eighteenth century, a booklet was published, entitled "Peri Ets Hadar," which includes a ritual based on the practices of the kabbalists. It lists many fruits which are to be eaten on this holiday, with special emphasis given to those grown in Israel. The booklet calls for the drinking of four cups of wine as at the traditional Passover seder. A prayer for the people of Israel is recited along with a number of Biblical passages which relate to fruit or vegetation.

According to the kabbalists, one should taste at least

twelve fruits on *Tu B'Shvat*. Moroccan Jews customarily eat a minimum of fifteen different fruits. Iraqi celebrations called for serving at least one hundred kinds of fruits, nuts and vegetables. The text for the occasion includes readings from the Bible, Zohar, and rabbinic writings. A festive meal follows the readings.

The four cups of wine drunk during the service each have their own significance. The first cup is pale white wine. This symbolizes winter and the dormant earth awaiting the planting season. The second cup is more golden in color and represents the time when the earth comes alive and sap starts to flow from the trees. The third cup of wine is a rose, symbolizing the blossoming of the trees. (In Israel, *Tu B'Shvat* is associated with the flowering of almond trees.) The final cup of wine is a deep red, symbolizing the land's ripening fruit and its overall fertility.

The Blessing of the Sun

Jewish tradition acknowledges a solar cycle, which takes 28 years. According to the Biblical account of creation, the sun was created on the fourth day—Wednesday—at the time of sunrise. The sun's yearly cycle takes 365 and a fourth days. Therefore, the position of the sun at the end of its first anniversary of existence was one-fourth of a day later than its position on the morning of its creation. Each year, it moves an additional quarter of a day. Thus it takes 28 years for the sun to return to the exact position in which it stood on the Wednesday morning when it was first created. A service and blessing commemorates the creation of the sun, once every 28 years at sunrise.

The service includes quotations from the Bible relating to the sun. Its main feature is the blessing which states: "Blessed are You, Lord our God King of the universe, Who performs the act of creation."

Jewish tradition, then, not only ties our spirituality to the daily rhythms of the sun, the monthly rhythms of the moon, the seasonal rhythms of nature, but also to a 28 year cycle of the sun.

Other Natural Phenomena

Jewish law prescribes a blessing upon seeing a falling star, on experiencing an earthquake, on witnessing lightning and thunder, on observing exceedingly strong winds. On all of these phenomena, the blessing is: "Blessed are You, Lord our God, King of the Universe, Who performs the act of creation." All of these natural phenomena are reflections of the original act of God's creation. An alternative blessing which may also be recited is: "Blessed are You, Lord our God, King of the universe, Whose strength and might fill the world." Rabbi David Abudarham explained that this blessing praises God who gives nature the power to reveal the ultimate power of the Creator of the universe. By seeing an image of God's strength in the powers of nature, we become awed by God's greatness. (The present custom is to recite the blessing "Who performs the act of creation" over lightning; and the blessing "Whose power and might fill the world," over thunder.)

The blessing praising God as the one who performs the act of creation is also recited on seeing an unusual mountain and a desert. These topographical phenomena hark back to the days of creation, and again remind the viewer of God, the Creator.

Upon seeing a rainbow, one should recite the following blessing: "Blessed are You Lord our God King of the universe Who remembers His covenant (with Noah), Who is trust-worthy in His covenant and established in His word." The Torah describes the rainbow as a sign of God's covenant with His creations on earth, that He will never again bring a flood to destroy humanity. It is interesting that God chose the rainbow as a sign for His permanent covenant with humans. A rainbow is intangible, unreachable, and ephemeral. God rests His covenant not in something solid and unshakable, but in a bodiless rainbow, a colorful bow of vapor refracted in the sunlight. God's power can be seen not only in great mountains and powerful oceans—but also in something as insubstantial and transient as a rainbow.

A Talmudic discussion about rainbows recognizes that this mysterious natural phenomenon is in some way a reflection of God Himself. Rabbi Abba stated that anyone who stares at a rainbow is showing disrespect for God (Hagigah 16a). The sage Rava said that anyone who stares at a rainbow is obligated to prostrate himself on the ground. These opinions are based on the verse in Ezekiel 1:28 which compares Ezekiel's vision of the brightness around God to the appearance of a rainbow. "As the appearance of the bow that is in the cloud in the day of rain, so was the appearance of the brightness round about, this was the appearance of the lightness of the glory of the Lord. And when I saw it, I fell upon my face and I heard a voice of one that spoke." The rainbow, therefore, is suggestive of the glory of God Himself, and should inspire within us a sense of awe and mystery.

Psalm 19

We return to the first verses of Psalm 19: "The heavens declare the glory of God, and the firmament tells His handiwork. Day unto day utters the tale, night unto night unfolds knowledge. There is no word, no speech, their voice is not heard, yet their course extends through all the earth, and their theme to the end of the world."

God is manifest in the world He created. The natural rhythms and natural phenomena are reflections of the greatness of the Creator. Jewish spirituality is intimately linked to the natural world, and through the natural world to God. Nature is filled with suggestions, symbols, invitations. The religious person is sensitive to these messages and responds to them with blessings and special observances. The Torah and the universe have the same Author.

2. CHANGED PERCEPTIONS

Jewish religious experience, as has been seen, is intimately linked to the rhythms of the natural world. The rhythms of the sun and moon govern our times of prayer, our religious festivals, our meditation of the universe. The phenomena of nature evoke within us responses to the greatness of God, the Creator, and we recite blessings on witnessing the powers of nature.

Centuries of Westernization and urbanization have profoundly affected Jewish religious sensitivity. There has been a steady and increasing alienation between Jewish religious observance and the natural world, with a parallel diminution in sensing the awe of God as Creator of the natural universe.

To illustrate the changed perception, we may consider the commonly observed Jewish religious experiences which recur on a regular basis. Modern Jews identify their religious lives with such events as the Passover seder, the High Holy Day synagogue services, Friday night Shabbat ceremonies and meal, the study of Torah, synagogue worship. The common denominator of these observances is that they generally happen *indoors*. They are observances in a synagogue, a home, or a place of study.

If we were to consider the situation of the ancient Israelites, we would be confronted with a different religious sensibility. The most important observances for them would have included the three pilgrimages to Jerusalem when they would

19

journey to the holy city to celebrate Passover, Shabuoth and Succoth. They would include the observance of *Bikkurim*, the bringing of the first fruits to the Temple, a ceremony which was a great outdoor celebration. They would include the festivities which took place during the harvest festivals, the sharing of harvests with the poor, the bringing of animals to Jerusalem to be offered as sacrifices. Almost everything, in fact, would have involved being outdoors, in contact with the natural world.

Obviously, we have moved a long way from the agricultural life of ancient Israel to the urban life of contemporary society. Our religious images and observances, the things we consider essential and meaningful, have been transformed over the generations due to the sociological and demographic changes. By urbanizing religion and by placing its most important events indoors, we have lost touch with the original religious insight which connected us with the rhythm of nature.

Jewish law often speaks in the old "natural" language. We have seen in the previous chapter how dependent religious life was on the natural order of the universe. But, today when we discuss the times of prayer, we speak not of sunrise or sunset so much as of specific times such as 7 a.m. or 6 p.m. etc. In former times, Jews knew that the Sabbath was concluded by going outside and looking for stars. If it was dark enough to be able to observe three stars, then the Sabbath was over. Today, calendars and synagogue schedules list the time when Sabbath ends with the arrogant precision of mathematics. A person may pray in the morning without having experienced sunrise; may pray in the afternoon, without having experienced sunset; may say evening prayers without having seen a star in the sky. Religious life can be celebrated indoors, with the assistance of clocks and calendars, without the need arising to go outside and determine the position of the sun.

By bringing religion indoors, some of our feeling of awe for the universe and its Creator has been lost. The regular daily connections with nature which Jewish tradition has prescribed are no longer easily experienced. But losing contact with the natural world threatens to make religion increasingly artificial, removed from its basic life source.

The Jewish ideal of a religious person has undergone a change over the centuries. Until relatively modern times, the ideal religious personality was one who spent much time outdoors, who contemplated the wonders of the universe and the wisdom of its Maker. The ideal Jew lived in harmony with nature and participated in its rhythms. The notion that ideal piety can be found in a pale, scholarly, undernourished saint who spends his days and nights studying Torah in a study hall is not true to the original Jewish religious vision. The Biblical heroes and prophets, the Talmudic sages, the medieval pietists and mystics—all were involved in outdoor religion.

Prayer and Windows

Attitudes on spirituality are suggested by the kind of windows used in places of worship. Windows are the connection between the indoor world and the world outside. The location and transparency of the windows indicate the extent to which worshippers are expected to relate to the world outdoors while they are engaged in prayer.

The Talmud (Berakhot 34b) records the opinion of Rabbi Hiyya bar Abba in the name of Rabbi Yohanan: "A person should not pray except in a house which has windows. . . ." The proof text is drawn from the Book of Daniel. Since Daniel offered his prayers while looking through a window in the direction of Jerusalem, so this precedent should be followed by subsequent generations. The commentator, Rabbi Shelomo Yitzhaki (Rashi) explains that "windows cause one to concentrate his heart, since he looks towards the heavens and his heart is humbled." According to this opinion, a person praying indoors may reach a higher spiritual level by looking out a window to see the heavens.

Yet, windows in synagogues have varied from place to place and generation to generation, reflecting different attitudes towards the outside world. In some synagogues, windows were built high up on the wall, above the height of any person. This was done in order to prevent people from being distracted from their prayers by letting their eyes wander to the outdoors during services. Windows, which serve to bring the outside in, also serve to connect the inside with the outside. If praying requires concentration on the words of the prayer, windows can be distracting. Indeed, a fear of the distraction of windows emerged in many communities. Windows, even when placed high up on the synagogue walls, were considered a necessary evil at worst, or at best a possible aid to prayer only in the event that one was unable to concentrate properly on his own. The commentary, Magen Abraham, on the Shulhan Arukh (O.H. 90:4) states that one's eyes should be directed downward during prayer. "Nevertheless, when one's concentration is broken, he can lift his eyes towards the heavens in order to awaken his concentration."

The fear of windows is evident in a feature common to almost all western synagogues: stained glass. The use of stained glass windows has a long history in Christian Europe, with great churches boasting artistic windows, some quite ancient. Apparently, European Jews were impressed by this feature of Christian religious architecture so that synagogues began to have stained glass windows too.

Stained glass windows, though they may be very beautiful, were not incorporated into religious architecture merely for the sake of beauty. The desire for artistic beauty could have been satisfied by tapestries, frescoes, wall carvings etc. Although generations of cultural conditioning have made us grow accustomed to stained glass windows in houses of worship, there is no intrinsic need for them from an aesthetic point of view. The windows reflect a philosophical attitude on prayer and our sense of spirituality.

Normally, windows exist to let the outside world enter

the world indoors. Stained glass windows, however, serve the opposite function: they keep the outside world *outside*. They protect the indoor world from intrusions from the outside.

Stained glass windows create an artificial world of indoor spirituality. Upon entering a synagogue with stained glass windows, for example, we enter a religious realm, a world unto itself without reference to anything outside. It is irrelevant where such a synagogue is actually located: it might be in the middle of New York City or in China or on top of a mountain or along a seashore. To a person inside the synagogue, the outside world is closed out; it cannot penetrate the colored windows.

The underlying motivation for creating such windows is the belief—whether acknowledged or not—that prayer can best be experienced in a place which is closed off from the distraction of the outside world. When one enters a synagogue with stained glass windows, one knows immediately that he is in a place of worship. The "inwardness" of the building makes its message known.

But there have been many synagogues, especially in non-Western countries, where the synagogue windows have been clear, where worshippers could see what was going on outside. In such synagogues, people could recite their prayers while also viewing the gardens, trees and other outdoor scenery. The synagogue of Rabbi Yosef Karo in Safed, for example, has clear windows through which one can see the wonderful mountainous scenery of the Galilee. Synagogues with clear windows reflect no fear of the outside world, no need to create an artificially enclosed structure for prayer to God.

Since the natural world and the spiritual world are organically connected, the Talmudic requirement of praying only in a house with windows makes much sense. But the windows should be clear; they should be an opening between the person praying and God, Creator of heaven and earth. Stained glass windows symbolize a changed sense of spirituality, a break from the traditional outdoor religiosity.

The windows in our houses of worship are also windows to our souls. They represent our attitudes towards the outside world, and towards the inside world, and towards the world inside each of us.

Natural Experience Versus Intellectual Abstraction

From infancy, we are taught what to ignore and what to notice. Our sensory organs receive numerous stimuli constantly, so we are trained to focus on specific stimuli rather than to deal with everything at one time. Our eyes focus on details, our ears listen for specific sounds and voices. We pay no attention to so many things which occur to us because we are trained to ignore them. Do you feel your heart beating? Do you feel the pressure of your feet as they rest on the ground? Do you see, hear, smell, feel or taste all the stimuli which assault you at this moment? No. It would be annoying if we could not control our sensory powers to some extent, in order to diminish the impact of stimuli on us when we neither want nor need them.

There are different ways of perceiving reality. Our senses are trained by our upbringing to relay what is considered important and to put aside things which are considered extraneous. For example, the Western mind focuses on objects, on solid forms, on individual people. The Eastern mind tends to absorb objects, solid forms and individual people in their relationship with space and with everything else around them. We are not, therefore, "objective" in our description of reality. To a large extent, we see and describe reality in the way our culture has taught us to do.[1]

This observation relates not only to our sensory perceptions but also to our ways of viewing history, religion, civilization. We tend to think in patterns that we have inherited, without realizing how our understanding is limited and biased.

For example, Western civilization places significant em-

phasis on intellectuality and analytical thinking. Greek philosophy has set the pattern for searching for truth, for scientific investigation, and for logical reasoning. Western tradition stresses systematic philosophy, with its orderliness and
abundance of proofs.

Western philosophical works, including works by Jewish thinkers, have been concerned with such questions as the
existence of God, epistemology, and ultimate Truth. Western
thinkers have developed systematic theology, with axioms,
proofs and logical demonstrations. Psychology and psychiatry have also developed in the West, reflecting this civilization's desire to understand everything in an analytic, scientific fashion. Even our own minds and thoughts are subjected
to the process of analysis.

Through centuries of Western influence, the discourses
of Jewish philosophy have adopted Western analytic methods. Jewish thinkers—Philo, Saadiah, Maimonides to name
only several—have attempted to present Judaism in a systematic and reasonable way. Jewish philosophers delineated
principles of the Jewish faith, elaborated on their meanings
and implications. They suggested a rational basis for the
commandments of the Torah. Yet, these features of Western
philosophy were not indigenous to Jewish thought. Rather,
they were adopted due to an outside influence. Moses and
Aristotle represent very different world views. Moses spoke
to God face to face. He did not need to prove the existence of
God or to provide any philosophical arguments for God's
reality. Aristotle, on the other hand, devised logical proofs to
demonstrate a First Cause, an unmoved mover. Moses experienced God as a living reality; and Aristotle could not
imagine speaking to God face to face. Whereas the Greek
philosophers engaged in philosophic speculation to find
Truth, the Biblical characters and prophets conversed with
God—the ultimate source of Truth—quite naturally and
calmly, as though it is a perfectly normal circumstance to
communicate with Him.

Western philosophy has difficulty understanding the Biblical world view. It can deal with proofs and systems; but it cannot deal seriously with spontaneous experiences, with revelations from God, with mystical insights. In order to understand the Jewish worldview on its own terms, we need to transcend the intellectual constraints imposed on our thinking by Western philosophy.

The Torah presents no philosophical arguments, no theological discourses. It speaks in its own idiom, with its own assumptions. Moses saw no need to present a systematic list of principles of faith. Jews lived for millenia without systematic philosophy and apparently felt no lack in their religious lives due to this absence of philosophy in the Western sense. The tradition of the Torah is a tradition of direct, "holistic" relationship with God. The tradition flows with the natural rhythms of the universe. The original truths of the Torah are in the domain of experience rather than speculation. The Torah is remarkably non-theological and non-philosophical, being primarily concerned with describing people in their relationships with each other and with God. Its concern is life rather than abstract thought.

Words of the Torah

Words are symbols which we use in order to communicate with each other. Words are not reality; they simply suggest a reality. For example, we may all agree to call a flat board resting on four legs a "table." But this object is not a table, but only something which we agree to call a table. It is actually a combination of atoms, energy and matter; it is, in fact, so complicated that it would be nearly impossible to describe everything about it. We simplify things by calling it a table, and we all understand what we are talking about.

When we use words which symbolize emotions, the words are approximations of feelings—not the feelings themselves. Our words are used as suggestions, analogies, intimations. No one can fully express his feelings or ideas, since something is lost in transforming these feelings and ideas into words, or other symbols such as art or music.

This dilemma was expressed by the famous 16th century mystic, Rabbi Isaac Luria, who lived in Safed. One of his students asked him why he did not write his teachings down in books. Rabbi Luria answered: "It is impossible, because all things are inter-related. I can hardly open my mouth to speak without feeling as though the sea burst its dams and over-flowed. How then shall I express what my soul has received, and how can I put it down in a book?" Experience and understanding are too vast; words are too inadequate.[2]

The word which is perhaps the ultimate symbol is "God." This word evokes deep feelings and ideas. Since it is impossible for us to express ourselves completely, we limit ourselves by using a word: God. When we say that God is just, or that God is merciful, we are using symbolic, suggestive language. "Just" and "merciful" are reflections of feelings we have (or would like to have) about the force which we call God. But no attribute of God is anything more than a sugges-tion or a wish, and no word truly expresses reality but only suggests reality.

The Torah, of course, is composed of words. God re-vealed Himself to the Israelites through words. He created the world through words. Yet, these words too—though divine in origin—are suggestive and symbolic. Rabbi Ishmael, one of the outstanding Talmudic sages, taught that the Torah speaks in the language of humans (Sanhedrin 64b). God conveyed something about Himself by means of words, sym-bols which could be meaningful to humans.

A Midrash relates that when God was preparing to give the Torah to the people of Israel, the angels in heaven argued that *they* themselves should be given the Torah, not the Israelites. God called Moses to heaven to answer the claim of the angels. Moses told the angels quite simply that the Torah was not relevant to them. Did they leave Egypt? Did they have jealousies so that they needed special commandments governing their behavior? Did they have parents to honor? In short, the text of the Torah related to Israel, not to angels. God was pleased with Moses' refutation of the angels' claim and therefore did give the Torah to Israel.

Rabbi Yosef Hayyim of Baghdad (late 19th–early 20th century) was bothered by this Midrash.[3] Didn't the angels know what was written in the Torah? Why did they make their claim in the first place? They should have realized that it was not relevant to them but only to the Israelites. Rabbi Yosef Hayyim resolved this difficulty with the following explanation. The words of the Torah have two levels of meaning—the *peshat*, the simple external meaning; and the *sod*, the hidden deeper meaning. The *peshat* indeed is not relevant to angels, but the *sod* is, and it was for the *sod* that they argued. The angels ignored the literal meaning of the words, seeing only their profound truths.

Rabbi Mosheh ben Nahman, one of the great medieval Sephardic mystics and commentators, notes in the preface to his commentary on the Torah: "We possess an authentic tradition showing that the entire Torah consists of the names of God, and that the words we read can be divided in a different way so as to form (God's) names . . . The statement in the aggadah that the Torah was originally written with black fire on white fire confirms our belief that the writing was continuous, without divisions into words, which made it possible for the Torah to be read either as a sequence of (God's) names or in the traditional way as history and commandments. The Torah as given to Moses was divided into words in such a way as to be read as divine commandments. But at the same time, he received the oral tradition, whereby it was to be read as a sequence of names."

The words of the Torah, then, may be understood on different levels. The words invite meditation and imagination. They are suggestions of deeper truths. A rabbinic legend had it that Rabbi Akiba was not only able to understand the symbolic meaning of the words of the Torah and each of its letters, but he also could interpret the ornamental crowns (*taggin*) which grace some of the letters of the Torah scroll. Since the Torah is a revealed text of God, its words—and even its ornamental crowns—are of profound significance.

When we attempt to understand the Torah and authentic Jewish spirituality, we need to be mindful of the strong cultural biases we have inherited from the Western philosophic tradition. The urbanization and Westernization of Jews over the past centuries have moved us away from the central religious insights of the Torah tradition. As we open our eyes more to the outdoors, to the rhythms of nature, we will come into relationship with God, Creator of the universe. The Torah and its words are guides to experience, symbols of undefined and undefinable truths. Jewish spirituality entails appreciating the value of calm, natural wisdom; and being aware of the limitations of abstract, analytic, systematic philosophy.

3. THE RHYTHMS OF TIME

Sacred Time

Mircea Eliade has observed in his book *The Sacred and the Profane* that human beings experience time on two levels. First and most obvious is "normal" time, the time contemporary with our lives. This kind of time is linear. It has a beginning—our birth; a middle—the years of our lives; and an end—our death. But there is also another kind of time which we experience, but which is not contemporary with our lives. This is sacred time, time contemporary with an original sacred event, the time of creation, the time of the "myths of the gods."

Eliade writes: "Hence religious man lives in two kinds of time, of which the most important, sacred time, appears under the paradoxical aspect of circular time, reversible and recoverable, a sort of eternal mythical present that is periodically reintegrated by means of rites."[1] Thus, a religious person does not live only in the historical present. He also experiences a return to a sacred time as it occurred *ab origine, in illo tempore.* The ceremonies of religious festivals serve the purpose of leading the religious person into that original sacred time.

Eliade has written that "the participants in the festival become contemporaries of the mythical event. In other words, they emerge from their historical time . . . and recover primordial time, which is always the same, which belongs to

eternity. Religious man periodically finds his way into mythical and sacred time, re-enters the *time of origin*, the time that
'floweth not' because it does not participate in profane temporal duration, because it is composed of an *eternal present*,
which is indefinitely recoverable."[2] A religious person enters this sacred and indestructable time.

The yearly calendar includes the same sacred festivals,
commemorating the same mythical events. Each year, the
religious person has the possibility of experiencing periodi-
cal returns to primordial situations by entering sacred time.
For religious people of the primitive and archaic societies, "it
is by virtue of this eternal return to the sources of the sacred
and the real that human existence appears to be saved from
nothingness and death."[3]

Eliade observes that Judaism offered a major innovation
over the archaic religions and over the ideal of eternal return
as elaborated in India and Greece. "For Judaism, time has a
beginning and will have an end. The idea of cyclic time is left
behind."[4] In other words, Judaism perceives time as being
linear rather than cyclical. Sacred events are part of normal
human history. In commemorating these events, the religious Jew does not re-enter the original sacred time, but only
experiences it as a historical memory.

Although Eliade's description of Judaism's innovation is
essentially valid, it must be said that Jews also experience
sacred time which involves a return to origins. Time is indeed linear; yet, historic flashbacks bring the religious Jew to
feel as though he experienced the primal religious events. In
fact, Jewish ritual's genius is in its demand to involve Jews in
a symbolic re-living of past events, not just intellectually
recounting them as historical phenomena. A consideration of
the Jewish festivals and religious commemorations will clarify the Jewish experience of sacred time.

High Holy Days

The Torah refers to the first day of the seventh month as a

day of sounding the shofar (ram's horn). The tenth day of the seventh month is designated as a day of atonement.

Jewish tradition has highlighted these days so that they have come to be known popularly as the High Holy Days or the Days of Awe (*Yamim Noraim*). The first day of the month is Rosh Hashanah, New Year, while the tenth day of the month is the fast day of Yom Kippur. Rosh Hashanah is generally observed in commemoration of God's creation of the world.[5]

The season of the High Holy Days is characterized by the belief that God stands in judgement of each of us during this period. He decides who will live and who will die, who will prosper and who will not, who will be healthy and who will be ill. The holidays are preceded by a month of *selihoth*, penitential prayers, when Jews ask for forgiveness for their sins, and assure God that they will do better during the coming year. Rosh Hashanah and Yom Kippur are solemn days of introspection, self-criticism and meditation on the meaning of one's life.

These themes are common to other ancient religions. Eliade has written that the new year was observed among ancient religions as a restoration of the primordial time, the pure time which existed at the moment of creation. "This is why the New Year is the occasion for 'purifications', for the expulsion of sins, of demons, or merely of a scapegoat. For it is not a matter merely of a certain temporal interval coming to its end and the beginning of another (as a modern man, for example, thinks); it is also a matter of abolishing the past year and past time. Indeed, this is the meaning of ritual purification; there is more than a mere 'purification'; the sins and faults of the individual and of the community as a whole are annulled, *consumed as by fire*."[6]

Yet, the Jewish observance of the New Year does not intend to transfer the religious Jew to the primordial time of Creation. Indeed, the early sages of Israel gave very little emphasis to the theme of God's creation of the universe on

the New Year. Interestingly, the Torah reading in the synagogue on Rosh Hashanah deals with Abraham's expulsion
of Ishmael and his binding of Isaac. It does not recount the
Creation story which opens the Torah in Genesis. The New
Year is surely a time to reflect about God as Creator of the
universe; but even more importantly, it is a time to reflect on
the meaning of life, the degree of our own faith and religious
commitment, and our connection to the people of Israel going back to our first forefather, Abraham. Although the Jewish New Year does have some of the elements of the New Year
as observed by ancient religions with cyclical time, the Jewish High Holy Days do not involve the return to the original
sacred time of Creation.

The Pilgrim Festivals

The three Biblical pilgrim festivals were originally connected to the harvest celebrations. But they were also associated with historical religious events.

Succoth commemorates the fact that the Israelites
dwelled in temporary booths (*succoth*) during their forty
years of wandering in the wilderness. They survived this
ordeal only through God's merciful providence. Succoth is
observed not by giving a historical lecture on the Israelites'
wanderings, but by the actual construction of booths in
which to dwell for the duration of the holiday. According to
Jewish law, the booths may not have closed roofs but should
be covered by loose branches or greens. During the festival,
Jews are supposed to consider the succah as their regular
home and to spend as much time as possible in it. One should
eat all his meals in the succah. In warm climates it has been
customary for people to sleep in it as well. These laws are
definite attempts to make Jews vicariously experience the
wanderings of the ancient Israelites. We literally live in the
same kind of temporary booths as our ancestors did; we want
to experience in some measure what they experienced. Our
observance makes us—at least in some way—contempora-

ries of the Israelites who experienced the original sacred time which gives meaning to this festival. Although the Jewish sense of time is linear, we have in this festival an example of a spiritual "flashback" where we try to relive and recapture the experience of our ancestors.

Pessah:

Pessah (Passover) celebrates the miraculous exodus of the Israelites from the slavery of Egypt. The Torah recounts how God appointed Moses and Aaron to represent the Israelites before Pharaoh. Pharaoh refused to free the Israelites, so the Egyptians suffered ten plagues, culminating with the death of the first born. The Israelites were spared from the ravages of these plagues. Finally, Pharaoh allowed the slaves to leave and the exodus began.

Once the Israelites had left, however, Pharaoh had a change of heart and sent his warriors after them. The Red Sea split before Moses and his people and all of them crossed safely to the other side. The Egyptians who pursued them were drowned as the sea came back together once the Israelites had passed through.

The festival of Pessah is observed by reliving vicariously the experiences of the ancient Israelites. For the duration of the holiday, Jews eat matsah, unleavened bread, rather than regular leavened bread. This is a reminder that the Israelites had no time to bake bread in their haste to leave slavery. Moreover, the matsah is symbolic of the bread of affliction which our ancestors ate while they were slaves.

On the first night of Pessah—or on the first two nights in the Diaspora—a special home service is held known as a seder. Aside from eating matsah, bitter herbs are also eaten to recall the bitter times suffered by our ancestors. Many Sephardic Jews have the custom of placing a piece of matsah in a sack and carrying it on their shoulders, as though they were among the Israelites of old carrying their belongings as they escaped from Egypt. The main text of the seder is the Haggadah, which recounts the exodus from Egypt and the great wonders performed by God on behalf of the people of Israel. The Haggadah states that in each generation, Jews are to feel as though they themselves participated in the exodus from Egypt. In other words, there is a clear attempt to recapture an ancient sacred time by reliving it in thought, symbol and vicarious experience.

Ostensibly, Pessah is a celebration of a historic event. Yet, it is not really history which makes this festival meaningful. On the contrary, the dominating feature is a national memory of an ancient event which is important not as a historical fact, but as a spiritual and emotional framework for our religious life.

That our main concern on Pessah is not pure history should be fairly obvious. In our recounting the story of the exodus, we do not provide a learned dissertation drawing on historical and archaeological sources. A great many details are omitted. The Biblical story itself is not presented in the style of historical scholarship. If our main concern on this festival is to recount history, then the Haggadah should read like a history text. It doesn't.

Professor Yosef Hayyim Yerushalmi, in his book *Zakhor*, has noted that historiography in the modern sense is something different from memory. Actually, it challenges memory. It discovers new facts and creates new perceptions. When we recount the story of the exodus of the Israelites, we are not engaging in the work of historians. Rather, we are sharing a historical national memory, and we are attempting to identify ourselves with our redeemed ancestors.

Yerushalmi points out a paradox. In the modern era, we have made incredible advances in uncovering the past and in advancing historical research. Yet, at the same time, our sense of continuity with the past has steadily declined. Hans Meyerhoff has noted: "Previous generations *knew* much less about the past than we do, but perhaps *felt* a much greater sense of identity and continuity with it."

Jews existed for millenia without scientific historians. The collective national memory provided continuity for all Jews in all places at all times. In blessing God in the Haggadah, we state that God has "redeemed us and redeemed our ancestors." We connect ourselves with those who have come before us. We have, in a sense, seen ourselves as being contemporaries of our ancestors. Put in other terms, the festival is an opportunity to experience sacred time. This experience is not provided by the intellect and reason; it is provided by national memory, by emotion and imagination, by a sense of continuity with family and ancestors.

Aside from the seder observances, other Pessah customs place us in a kind of sacred time. The Torah reading for the seventh day of Pessah is the description of the crossing of the Red Sea, and includes the moving song which Moses and the people of Israel sang upon their redemption. Also, on the night on which the festival concludes, it is customary among some Sephardic communities for parents and grandparents to return home from the synagogue, while their children and grandchildren eagerly await them. With great joy, with singing and gladness, the parents and grandparents open the door to the home, and throw handfuls of coins, candy and grass, and all the children scramble to collect the treasures. The custom harks back to the joy which the Israelites experienced upon crossing the Red Sea. The coins are reminders of the fact that the Egyptians gave the Israelites gold and silver before the exodus began. The grass recalls the reeds along the Red Sea. The candy, which is generally a symbol of sweetness and happiness, may also call to mind the mannah which God provided to the Israelites after they crossed the Red Sea.

These customs and observances help one to transcend the present time in order to participate in a sacred time. While never losing awareness of the present, we also share the emotions, feelings and thoughts of our ancestors in their original relationship with God.

Shabuoth

The festival of Shabuoth, which occurs seven weeks after the second night of Pessah, was originally celebrated as a harvest festival. It has the added historical association of being the time when God revealed the Ten Commandments to the children of Israel at Mount Sinai. The festival is only one day in Israel, two days in the Diaspora. Many religious Jews stay up all night on the evening of Shabuoth in order to study Torah. This custom is a symbolic gesture in which Jews demonstrate their total love and commitment to the Torah, God's revealed word. Interestingly, it was at one of these all-night study vigils on the eve of Shabuoth that the famous 16th century scholar and mystic, Rabbi Yosef Karo, received a personal divine revelation through a "maggid," an angelic voice.

On the morning of Shabuoth, the Torah reading in the synagogue is the section of Exodus describing the revelation at Sinai. The prophetic portion is the beginning of the book of Ezekiel, in which the prophet describes his vision of God on His throne of glory. The intention of these readings is to draw us into the experience of revelation.

Commemorations

The Jewish calendar includes a number of days which commemorate ancient happenings. In each case, Jews are expected to participate in sacred time, not merely to understand intellectually the details which are the reason for the commemoration.

For example, the holiday of Hanukkah celebrates the victory of the Maccabees over the Hellenistic Syrians in the second century B.C.E. Tradition has it that when the Maccabees regained control of the Temple in Jerusalem, they wished to light the Menorah—the seven branched candelabrum of the Temple. But they found only one jar of pure oil with enough fuel to last one day. Miraculously, that oil lasted eight days, giving the people enough time to make new pure oil. In celebration of Hanukkah, Jews are obligated to light a Menorah in their homes on each of the eight nights of the festival. The lights are to be lit near a window, so that people walking in the street can see them and be aware of the wonderful miracle which occurred to the Jewish people. A special paragraph is added in the silent devotion of the three daily prayers, as well as in the Grace after Meals, in which God is praised for having given victory to the small, valiant Israelite army which faced such a formidable foe. The significance of this festival is not in the precise historical details of the Maccabean revolution, but rather in the emotional, nationalistic memories. The holiday has always been a source of encouragement to Jews who have faced enemies of great strength and number. The Maccabees proved that a small faithful group of Jews could defeat seemingly more powerful enemies. The lighting of the Hanukkah candles is a yearly reminder of God's providence over Israel, and of Israel's devotion to its religious freedom and national identity.

The festival of Purim celebrates the salvation of the ancient Persian Jewish community through the leadership of Mordecai and Esther. The king's advisor, Haman, received the king's approval for a plan to destroy all the Jews in his kingdom. Instead, the Jews were saved and Haman himself was hanged. To celebrate this day, Jews read the scroll of Esther, the vivid Biblical narrative recounting the Purim story. One of the obligations of the day is to have a festive meal, in order to enjoy the happiness of the day. It is also incumbent upon Jews to give charity to the poor and to send gifts of food to friends and neighbors on Purim. These obligations teach the importance of sharing and caring for others. They create good will in the community. Purim, thus, becomes not merely a day for remembering an ancient redemption of Jews, but also a day for joy and happiness within contemporary Jewish communities.

The Jewish calendar includes a number of fast days commemorating sad events which occurred to the Jewish people in the past. The most dramatic of these fast days is the ninth of the month of Av. This day is traditionally associated with the destruction of both the First and Second Temples in Jerusalem. Following the destruction of the Second Temple by the Romans in 68 C.E., the Jews lived in exile for nearly nineteen hundred years before regaining sovereignty in the land of Israel.

The ninth of Av is observed by fasting the complete day, from before sunset on the eve of the ninth until after sunset on the ninth. Customs of mourning are kept, such as not wearing leather shoes, sitting on the floor, avoiding social conversation. The prayer services are characterized by melancholy melodies, the chanting of dirges and laments. The day closes with a note of consolation, with readings from the prophet Isaiah in which God promises to restore Israel to its former glory. As with the other sacred times discussed earlier, the purpose of this day is not to gain academic knowledge about historical events, but rather to share the sacred time in which those events occurred. The key to understanding these holidays and commemorations is in the realm of experience, emotion, memory; not in reason, scientific research, or overintellectualization.

Sabbath

The holiest of Jewish holy days is Shabbat, the Sabbath. It begins at sunset on Friday evening and ends after sundown on Saturday night.

The holiness of Shabbat is not observable objectively. Unlike Rosh Hodesh or the seasonal festivals, there is no clear pattern in the natural world which would indicate that the seventh day of every week should be considered sacred. There is no scientifically observable difference between time on the Sabbath and time on any other day of the week. The day is sacred and noteworthy only to those who are spiritually attuned to its sanctity.

Shabbat is a commemoration of God as Creator. The Torah opens with the account of creation in which God created the world in six stages and on the seventh stage He rested. Likewise, we symbolically acknowledge this process of creation by working on six days and resting on the seventh. Thus, Shabbat becomes an expression of our recognition of the original rhythm of God's act of creation.

The intentional desecration of Shabbat is considered by the Torah to be a capital offense. The Talmud and Jewish law consider one who has willfully violated the Sabbath to be in the same category as one who has worshipped idols. By desecrating Shabbat, one denies that God created the universe and that God Himself sanctified the seventh day as Shabbat. Since this concept is so fundamental to Jewish belief, one who discards it intentionally has separated himself from the people of Israel and the God of Israel.

On Shabbat, one is obliged to abstain from 39 types of creative activity, such as building, plowing, writing, sewing etc. These endeavors reflect human control of nature. For six days of each week, we are empowered to mould the natural world to meet our needs—to build, to plow, to cut and shape. We light fires, transport merchandise. On Shabbat, though, we abstain from these weekday activities. We recognize, not just by philosophical meditation but by symbolic emulation, that God is the sole Creator and Master of the universe. On the seventh day, when we are not engaged in controlling the natural world, the natural world continues to be sustained by God's power. It is a lesson in humility for humans to realize that they are not the ultimate controllers of the natural world.

But Shabbat is not merely a day to abstain from certain kinds of activity. It is also a day for the positive experience of joy, family togetherness, communal inter-relatedness. Shabbat is sanctified in the home with the lighting of candles before sunset, the eating of three festive meals during Shabbat, the singing of hymns around the family table. Shabbat is also sanctified in the synagogue—the prayer services of the day, the studying of Torah in the synagogue, the reaffirming of friendships.

Jewish law and custom prescribe that the Shabbat must be respected by wearing nice clothes, by preparing special foods, by studying Torah, and by participating in communal prayer. By changing our accustomed ways, we leave profane time and enter the sacred time of Shabbat.

Rabbi Eliezer Azikri, a 16th century Sephardic mystic, has explained in his book "Sefer Hareidim" that the three meals which are eaten in honor of Shabbat relate to the three major themes of the day.[8] The Friday night meal relates to the Shabbat of Creation, when God had completed the work of creating the universe in six days and then sanctified the seventh day. The blessing over wine on Friday evening which precedes the Shabbat meal is introduced with the chanting of the Biblical verses describing that first Shabbat of creation. The meal of Shabbat morning is connected to the Shabbat laws as revealed to the children of Israel on Mount Sinai. The morning prayer in the synagogue also makes reference to the fact that Shabbat was given as a commandment to the children of Israel by God at Sinai. The Shabbat afternoon meal is related to the "world that is all Shabbat," the future Messianic period. This theme, too, is central to the afternoon prayer which refers to God as being One and His name One, an allusion to Messianic times when everyone will recognize the true One God.

Kabbalists have attached great importance to yet a fourth meal, one that is served after Shabbat has already ended. This is known as the "Melaveh Malkah," the escorting of the Shabbat Queen. Just as the Shabbat Queen is welcomed on Friday evening with the Lekha Dodi hymn, so she is to be properly escorted on her departure.

At the conclusion of Shabbat, a special ceremony known as Havdalah (separation) symbolizes the return to non-sacred time. A blessing is recited over wine and over the fragrance of spices, herbs or fruit. Then a blessing is made over the light of a candle with several wicks, indicating that we may once again create fire and return to the regular tasks of the six work days. The Havdalah concludes with a blessing praising God for having separated between the holy and the profane, between light and darkness, between Israel and the nations, and between the Shabbat and the six work days. The sacred time of Shabbat, then, is set off at the beginning with the lights of the Shabbat candles and at the end with the fire of Havdalah. The time between these fires is categorically different from the profane time of the rest of the week. But no one can experience that sacred time unless he or she enters it consciously and with spiritual awareness.

In considering the sacred times of the Jewish people, we have seen that they involve a vicarious experience of primordial religious events. The symbols of the festivals and the Sabbath bring us back to the time of the creation of the world and to the major events of the ancient Israelites—exodus, revelation. Jewish traditions make one reminisce about those original events, even to feel as though one were somehow part of them. Yet, even in the midst of experiencing sacred time, the religious Jew does not surrender himself completely to those ancient events. Judaism does not let one lose consciousness of the present time, the linear time which runs from creation through history and to ultimate redemption. One may experience vicariously the original religious events; but one must always realize that he cannot actually return to them, that time is not cyclical.

We remember the past, we participate in it through symbol and thought. But we remain distinctly in the here and now, fully conscious of the unfolding of history.

4. | SACRED PLACES

Paradox and Terror

The Western mind has been troubled by the fact that humans are paradoxical beings. On the one hand, we are part of the natural world. Our bodies function like those of other animals; we go through the process of birth, life, decay and death. On the other hand, human beings have a "symbolic identity" which lifts us sharply out of nature. Ernest Becker, in his thoughtful volume *The Denial of Death*, has argued that a person "is a symbolic self, a creature with a name, a life history. He is a creator with a mind that soars out to speculate about atoms and infinity, who can place himself imaginatively at a point in space and contemplate bemusedly his own planet. This immense expansion, this dexterity, this ethereality, this self-consciousness gives to man literally the status of a small god in nature, as the Renaissance thinkers knew."[1]

Becker has called this existential paradox the condition of "individuality within finitude". He has contended that "in recent times every psychologist who has done vital work has made this paradox the main problem of his thought."

The result of this existential paradox, according to Becker, is terror. "Man is literally split in two: he has an awareness of his splendid uniqueness in that he sticks out of nature with a towering majesty, and yet he goes back into the ground a few feet in order blindly and dumbly to rot and disappear forever. It is a terrifying dilemma to be in and to have to live with." Lower animals are spared from this paradox, since they lack self-consciousness and anxiety about death. They simply live day by day as natural organisms. But since humans have a mind which can think abstractly, which gives a person a sense of his own identity, the prospect of being limited by a body and of dying creates dread.

Perhaps the terror to which Becker refers does not stem from the consciousness of death per se. Rather, it may derive from a person's feeling of meaninglessness. If one feels that his life has no value, no ultimate meaning—then death indeed can seem frightening. If life has no meaning, death becomes a meaningless end to a meaningless existence. Since Western society stresses individuality, fame, success etc., death becomes a nasty obstacle which prevents us from continuing to gain fame, wealth, power. And if life has no transcendent meaning, then death is ugly and terrifying.

Non-Western Jewish tradition has not been overly concerned with the dualism and terror posited by Becker and others. To be sure, there has long been an awareness of the existential paradox of human life. In Psalm 8, the Psalmist has expressed the problem. "When I look up at Your heavens, the work of Your fingers, the moon and the stars set in their places by You—what is man that You should be mindful of him, a mortal being that You should care for him? Yet You have made him a little lower than angels, crowning him with glory and honor." The dilemma is an integral part of human existence. Yet, the religious person need feel no terror or anxiety because of it. One can live with paradox and still remain calm.

What is a human's place in the eternity of time and the vastness of space? The span of human life is infinitesimal compared to eternity. Our greatest achievements are ultimately insignificant and transient. Even if our fame can last for a thousand years or five thousand years or ten thousand years—what is that compared to the endlessness of time? The

Jewish prayer book expresses this truth in a passage read very early in the morning service: "What are we? What is our life? What our goodness? What our righteousness? What our help? What our strength? What our power? What can we say in Your presence, Lord our God, God of our fathers? Are not the mightiest as naught before You, men of renown as if they were not, the wise as if without knowledge, the intelligent as if lacking in understanding? For our doings are often confusion, and the days of our life as vanity before You."

Jewish religious tradition deals with this dilemma in several ways. We have seen in the first chapter that Jewish spirituality is linked to the rhythms of nature. The natural world is an expression of God, the Creator. Even if we are awed by the vastness of nature and the greatness of God, we are also drawn closer to nature and to God. The alienation and fear give way to humility and love.

To speculate about the meaning of our lives in the face of eternity is depressing—and useless. Religious tradition attempts to keep alive one's sense of wonder, while at the same time making one feel more comfortable with his existential reality. Since we have the possibility of experiencing a spiritual relationship with the eternal God, life does have meaning; spiritual fulfillment can be attained.

Sacred time gives us the possibility of sharing eternity, of bringing time into humanly comprehensible terms. And since the universe is so vast that a person might feel like an atom in an endless physical cosmos, religion has the concept of sacred space. By designating particular places as being sacred, the religious person can live within his allotted space with meaning and dignity.

Sacred Space

The Torah records the dream of Jacob in which he saw a ladder connecting heaven and earth, with angels ascending and descending its steps. When he awoke from his dream, Jacob said: "Surely the Lord is in this place; and I knew it not." Jacob was frightened. He said: "How full of awe is this place. This is none other than the house of God, and this is the gate of heaven." Jacob took the stone which he had used as a pillow and set it up as a pillar, and poured oil on top of it. He named that place Beth-El, the house of God (Genesis 28:16-19).

The ladder in Jacob's dream symbolizes the connection between the physical world and the spiritual world, between the finitude of matter and the infinity of spirit. These two seemingly opposite domains are connected and related to each other. At the instant of that recognition, Jacob recognized that he was in a special place, a sacred place, where God had revealed Himself to him. Jacob's immediate response was to take a simple rock, upon which he had rested his head when he slept, and sanctify it, making it a symbol of God's presence on earth. Certainly, God cannot be limited to a particular stone or any other specific place. God transcends space, just as He transcends time. Yet, Jacob consecrated the place so that this physical space was also "the gate of heaven."

The story dramatically demonstrates a key feature of religious understanding and experience. While God cannot be limited to a particular space, yet a human being can set aside a place and recognize it to be sacred, a point of connection between himself and the Almighty God. Human understanding cannot comprehend the vastness of God without being overcome with overwhelming fear and trembling. But a sacred space, being limited and comprehensible, enables one to deal with the physical universe and with God.

Of course, the entire universe is sacred since it is a manifestation of God's will and power. Yet, by designating a special sanctity to specific places, the religious person creates a new spiritual reality, a new gate to heaven. Sacred and non-sacred space may appear objectively to be the same; but within the mind of a religious person, they are different kinds of worlds.

Threshold

Mircea Eliade has described a threshold as "the limit, the boundary, the frontier that distinguishes and opposes two worlds and at the same time the paradoxical place where those worlds communicate, where passage from the profane to the sacred world becomes possible."[2] It is not surpirsing, therefore, that the threshold is a place of significance in the traditions of many peoples.

Since the home is the main base of human life, it occupies a special, private kind of space, different from the public domain outside. The Torah has commanded that the threshold of a Jewish home be graced with a mezuzah, an encased piece of parchment inscribed with the first two paragraphs of the Shema. The mezuzah is not an amulet or a good luck charm. Its purpose is to differentiate clearly between the outside domain, and the sacred, private domain of the home. By seeing the mezuzah whenever one enters or leaves his home, one is reminded of the presence of God and the commandments of His Torah. Among some Jews, the custom has arisen to place one's hand on the mezuzah upon entering and leaving home, and then to kiss his fingers. This is a way of consciously absorbing the message of the mezuzah as one passes from one kind of space to another.

The Home

The Jewish home should reflect sanctity. It should contain sacred books. It should be the place where family members study Torah together, where they deepen their emotional connections to each other and to their tradition.

The table upon which the family eats is compared to an altar of God. It demands respect, blessing before and after meals, appropriate conversation at mealtime.

It is customary among many Jews to have a special wall hanging which is hung on an eastern wall. This is to remind the family of the direction of Jerusalem when they pray at home.

A Jewish home is a sacred place.

The Synagogue and Study Hall

Buildings dedicated to prayer and the study of Torah are considered by Jewish tradition to be sacred places. The world inside these buildings is qualitatively different from the world outside.

The Shulhan Arukh, the classic code of Jewish law, has a special section on the sanctity of the synagogue (Orah Hayyim 151). The laws indicate the separateness and specialness of these sacred structures. It is forbidden to act in a light-headed fashion in synagogues and study halls. Silly laughter, extraneous conversation, eating and drinking are forbidden in these holy precincts. One is not supposed to enter them in order to get out of the sun or out of the rain, since these places are not to be used simply for one's convenience. Even funerals are not to take place in synagogues, except in the case of outstanding rabbis and communal leaders. One is not allowed to use the synagogue or study hall as a pathway; but if he has to pass through these buildings, he must stop to read some sacred literature.

The sanctity of these buildings is not only exemplified by the rules of behavior in them. Their actual physical structures are accorded sanctity. For example, the Shulhan Arukh notes that it is customary to keep synagogues and study halls clean and to light candles in them as a sign of honor. Even after sacred buildings have been destroyed, they retain their holiness. Just as we are obligated to treat them respectfully when they are standing, so we are obligated to honor them even when they are in ruins. If grass and weeds are growing out of the ruins, we are not allowed to pull them out; rather, we must let them continue to grow in order to create within us a sense of sadness. This will inspire us to rebuild the buildings as soon as possible, rather than to leave them in a state of ruin.

Interestingly, the study hall is considered to be more sacred than the synagogue. If a community decides to convert its synagogue into a study hall, they may do so since they are elevating the holiness of the building. However, if they wish to convert a study hall into a synagogue, they may not do so. Torah study is a more sacred value than prayer.

Cemetery

In Jewish tradition, the cemetery has the features of constituting sacred space. The land of the cemetery is considered to be consecrated; to be denied burial in a Jewish cemetery is a serious punishment for a religiously sensitive Jew.

According to the ancient laws of purity enumerated in the Torah, a priest (cohen) is not allowed to enter the precinct of a cemetery except in the case of burial of a near relative. Everyone who enters a cemetery becomes ritually unclean and must undergo a ritual purification. Today, the practice is to wash one's hands after leaving a cemetery. The laws of purity are a clear signal that the cemetery occupies a different kind of space from the territory outside its boundaries. It has the paradoxical status of being both consecrated, and, at the same time, a source of ritual impurity.

That a cemetery is held to be sacred space is evident even from popular language usage. If tombstones are thrown over or defaced, if the land of a cemetery is treated disrespectfully, we say that the cemetery has been "desecrated." Moreover, our behavior in a cemetery reflects the belief that this is a separate, special segment of space. Jewish tradition prescribes that one should not eat in a cemetery, nor act in a light-headed manner. The cemetery is the place for burial of people who have died, and also for holy books and objects that have become too worn out to be used. Thus, the cemetery is a place for reverence.

Among North African Jews, there arose a custom known as "hiloula." This is an annual pilgrimage to the grave of a saintly person. It was believed that the spirit of a righteous person continued to exert influence on the living. For example, there is an annual hiloula at the grave of Rabbi Amram ben Diouan in Asjen, Morocco. Rabbi Amram was an 18th century Israeli sage who travelled to Morocco to raise funds for the Jewish communities in the Holy Land. While on his travels, his son became deathly ill. Rabbi Amram prayed that his son's life be spared, and volunteered his own life as a substitute for that of his son. And so it was: Rabbi Amram died and his son recovered. His saintliness and his ability to intercede with the Almighty made a great impression on the Jews of Morocco, and his grave became venerated.

At a hiloula, bonfires are lit, passages of mystical texts are read, and prayers are offered. The general mood is festive rather than somber, but the underlying message of the event is to stress the eternal value of saintliness. Death does not end one's spiritual influence on earth.

As an act of personal devotion, many people have the custom of visiting graves of parents or other close relatives, especially during the week before Rosh Hashanah. These visits have a religious quality to them and further underscore the sense of sanctity which pervades a cemetery.

Personally Sacred Places

The Talmud (Berakhot 54a) teaches that we are obligated to recite a blessing when we see a place where miracles were performed for our ancestors. These places call to mind God's providence and are therefore to be treated with awe and devotion. The blessing praises God "Who performed miracles for our ancestors in this place." Likewise, if one comes to a place where a miracle has happened to him personally, he should recite a blessing to God "Who has performed for me a miracle in this place." Children and grandchildren should also say a blessing where a miracle happened to their parents and grandparents (Shulhan Arukh O.H. 218).

Some sages who were saved from danger had the custom of observing the anniversary of their salvation with meditation and thanksgiving prayers to God. They celebrated this occasion with friends and relatives in order to highlight the significance of the event. Moses Maimonides had the custom of spending the day in meditation on an anniversary of a near catastrophe, and on the next day he would rejoice.[3] These anniversary observances took place even though one did not actually return to the site where the miracle occurred. The sanctity of the place was acknowledged even if one was not able to be there.

Israel, the Holy Land

Jewish tradition ascribes holiness to the land of Israel, in distinction to all other lands in the world. This is evident from the widespread custom of Jews arranging for burial in Israel; or of placing some earth from Israel in the coffin of one who is buried outside Israel. There is a deep, mystical belief that even in death a Jew should be associated with the special holiness of the land of Israel.

Jewish law distinguishes between Israel and the other lands. This is especially true in the agricultural laws outlined in the Torah. The tithes, gifts to the priests (terumah), first fruits, the sabbatical year, the jubilee year—all these laws apply by Torah law only to land of Israel. Jews involved in agriculture outside of Israel are generally exempted from these rules. Since they do not share in the sanctity of the land of Israel, they do not share in the specific commandments relating to the land.

Because the land of Israel is sacred, the Talmud has lengthy discussions to determine the exact boundaries of Israel. Which territories are included in the holiness and which are excluded? Since ancient Syria adjoined Israel, and since many Jews lived in that adjacent land, some of the agricultural laws of Israel were also extended to Syria. Yet, living within the boundaries of Israel is considered to be a fulfillment of a Biblical commandment.

Jerusalem

Jerusalem is known in Jewish liturgy as "ir hakodesh," the holy city. Throughout the ages, Jews have made pilgrimages to Jerusalem and have felt that this is the city par excellence for sanctity. Jews pray facing in the direction of Jerusalem.

Within Jerusalem, the location of the ancient Temple is the holiest area. Within the Temple precincts, there were gradations of sanctity, the highest being "the holy of holies," a section where the high priest entered only once a year, on Yom Kippur. Popular Jewish tradition has identified the location of the Temple as being the same site where Abraham was prepared to offer his son Isaac as a sacrifice. So this place has very profound religious significance to religious Jews.

We have seen, then, that not all places share the same degree of sanctity. A religious Jew lives in a world dotted with sacred spaces. The physical universe, for all its vastness, is not terrifying but awe-inspiring. There are landmarks which serve as bridges between the physical world and the spiritual world. These sacred places are very much like the ladder in Jacob's dream: they are rooted in the ground, but they are at the same time the gates of heaven.

5. | RHYTHMS OF EVERYDAY LIFE

The normal rhythms of daily activity are linked by Jewish tradition to spirituality. God, as Creator and Providential Provider, is called to mind throughout the day. The religious person lives simultaneously in the world of reality and a world of transcendence. Everything reflects deeper meanings.

A verse in Psalm 16 has been a religious guide to Jews for centuries: "I set the Lord always before me." Jewish mystics have used this verse as the theme for a special prayer design which has been incorporated in their prayer books, and which has also been used as a wall hanging. Known as "Shiviti," (I have set . . .) this design is believed to have tremendous spiritual power, elevating the worshipper to a high level of awareness of God. Its power does not necessarily stem from the combination of words or the type of design: rather, it serves to remind the individual that God is always near him, always available, always watching. This consciousness of God's presence is a basic feature of Jewish religious life.

Another verse (Proverbs 3:6), teaches a similar lesson. "In all your ways know Him." Knowledge of God is an omnipresent responsibility. Heightening one's awareness of God, even in the humdrum activities of daily life, is a challenge which Jewish tradition meets in a variety of ways.

In the fifth chapter of his Introduction to the "Ethics of the Fathers," Maimonides states the Jewish attitude clearly. "A person should always place before his eyes one goal,

55

namely the understanding of the Name blessed be He, according to the ability of a person to know this." All of a person's activities should be directed to this single goal. One's eating, drinking, intercourse, sleeping, waking—all should be with the aim of strengthening one's body. The purpose of good health is to help one devote more effort to wisdom and to spiritual pursuits. And the purpose of these is to help one attain a deeper understanding of God. Maimonides notes that very few people can reach this level where their every activity is directly linked to knowledge of God; yet this is the goal for which to strive. One who reaches it approaches the level of the prophets.

The codes of Jewish law teach that one's actions should be "for the sake of Heaven." The daily rhythms of human life are intertwined with the daily rhythms of religious life.

Waking and Sleeping

Upon awakening, one should recite: "I thank You, ever-living divine King, that in Your love You have awakened my soul within me. Great is Your trustworthiness."[1] Just as we open our eyes, as we regain our consciousness after emerging from sleep, we immediately express gratitude to God for having awakened us and restored to us our soul, our consciousness. We recognize God's constant vigilance over us.

The Talmudic sages prescribed a number of blessings to be recited upon arising in the morning. Although these blessings are often recited in synagogue today at the beginning of morning services, they were originally to be recited in connection with the activities of getting up. The first blessing praises God for having given the rooster the ability to distinguish between night and day. This was to be said when one heard the crow of the rooster in the morning. Subsequent blessings praise God for the progressive stages in our awakening and getting ready for the new day: for opening our eyes, for allowing us to rise from bed, for straightening up our bodies when we stand, for clothing us, for making solid ground upon which we can walk, for arranging our steps, for caring for all our needs, for girding us, for crowning Israel with glory (a reference to tefillin).

The above blessings are preceded by a paragraph which acknowledges that God created our soul in purity and will one day take it back and restore it to us in the World to Come. The paragraph ends with a blessing to God "Who returns souls to dead corpses." The meaning of this blessing is that we compare our sleeping body with a dead body. During sleep, it is as though we have given our soul to God for safekeeping. When we awaken, it is as though the soul is returned to our body which until then has been "dead." This blessing underscores our absolute dependence on God for our very lives.

Upon awakening we thank God for restoring our soul to us; upon going to sleep we pray that God will protect us during our sleep and return us to life in the morning. Before reciting the Shema which declares the unity of God (and which is supposed to be recited by a dying person just before death), we say a little prayer which includes the following words: "May it be Your will to lay me down in peace and to raise me up again to happy and peaceful life with my portion in Your Torah. . . . Lighten my eyes again that I sleep not the sleep of death."

The prayers upon waking and going to sleep reflect the keen awareness of the finitude of human life in contrast to the Almighty and Eternal God. When a human being really knows that he is mortal, that he is dependent on God for his life—he lives his life in a religious spirit. He is not apt to be arrogant about his self-importance. Humility leads to a calmness about one's own life, and a greater tolerance for the lives of others.

Ridding One's Wastes

A natural function of the human organism is to rid its wastes. This activity occurs to everyone throughout the course of the day. In our culture, it is associated with privacy and perhaps even a degree of shame. We have developed a variety of euphemisms and slang words to describe the perfectly natural function of ridding our wastes.

Our sensitivity to this part of our lives is understandable. Ridding our wastes is the ultimate reminder of our biological existence. In the words of Ernest Becker, "execreting is the curse that threatens madness because it shows man his abject finitude, his physicalness, the likely unreality of his hopes and dreams."[2] It is difficult to imagine oneself as being in the image of God when he is in the process of excreting.

Jewish tradition has certainly been aware of this ambiguity of feeling towards ridding one's wastes. Yet, it has seen in this very mundane, biological function another sign of God's providence and wisdom. A blessing is to be recited after one has voided himself and then washed his hands. "Blessed are You, Lord our God, King of the universe. In wisdom You have formed humans, creating within them innumerable channels. In Your sublimity You know that were they rent or obstructed we could not subsist even for a short while. Blessed are You, Lord, Who works the miracle of healing for all flesh." So Jewish spiritual life also includes the rhythm of ridding our wastes.

Clothing

Jewish law and custom prescribe modest dress for men and women. Moreover the Torah includes several laws specifically relating to clothes. It prohibits wearing clothing which has been woven from wool and flax. Known as "shaatnez," this mixture of material seems to have no intrinsic quality which warrants this prohibition. It is generally regarded as a *hok*, a divine law which has no reason apparent to human understanding. Yet, the general prohibition can be understood as a way of making us conscious of the type of clothes we wear. Since clothing is such a basic human necessity, our concern with "shaatnez" keeps our religious awareness intact even when we make, buy or wear clothes.

Another interesting law of the Torah prescribes that *tsitsith*, fringes, be attached to the corners of four-cornered garments. The laws of *tsitsith* are extensive and we will not go into them here. However, the Torah teaches that the purpose of the *tsitsith* is to serve as a reminder of all God's commandments. By looking at them, one immediately remembers the Torah's instructions—and it is one's own clothes that serve this vital function.

In Biblical times, the *tsitsith* included one blue thread along with seven white ones. The Hebrew phrase "ur'item oto," is generally thought to mean "and you will see it (the *tsitsith*)" and thereby remember God's commandments. The talmudic sage, Rabbi Meir was puzzled by the word "oto," a singular term. The phrase should have read "otam," in the plural. He commented, therefore, that the verse is actually teaching that one who fulfills the commandment of tsitsith is considered to have received the Divine Presence, since the blue of the *tsitsith* resembles the sea, and the sea resembles the sky, and the sky resembles the Throne of Glory. The word "oto" refers to the single strand of blue in the *tsitsith*. (*Sifri* on Numbers 15:39) Some commentators have understood the word "oto" as deriving from the Hebrew word "ot" meaning "sign." According to this understanding, the verse is teaching that one who sees the *tsitsith* is seeing the sign of God, or God's seal. To have such a sign affixed to one's clothes is amazingly significant and impressive. Even our clothes lead us to a relationship with God.

Eating

One of the most basic rhythms of daily life is eating. Humans eat in order to maintain their bodies; but also to provide pleasure to themselves. The preparation of food so that it is pleasant to eat and to behold has played an important part in human civilization since antiquity. Food has a biological role in our lives, and also a social meaning.

Since we need food to sustain our lives, Jewish tradition

has a blessing upon eating every type of food. These blessings reflect the awareness that it is God who provides us with our sustenance. They are not so much statements of thanksgiving as of awe at God's greatness. For example, the blessing for bread is: "Blessed are You, Lord our God, King of the universe, Who brings forth bread from the earth." God gives the earth power to produce grain which can be made into bread. The blessing on fruit praises God "Who creates the fruit of the trees." The blessing on vegetables lauds God "Who creates the produce of the earth." The blessing over foods that do not derive from vegetation (i.e. meat, milk, water etc.) praises God since "all came into being through His word."

Not only are blessings to be recited before eating, but a grace should be recited after eating as well. The full grace after meals is recited upon concluding a meal in which one has eaten bread. A shorter grace is pronounced after eating certain fruits, baked goods (other than bread), and after drinking wine. After eating other things, the following blessing is to be recited: "Blessed are You, Lord our God, King of the universe, Creator of souls innumerable and their needs; for all that You have created to keep every living soul in life, blessed is the everlasting God."

These blessings praise God for maintaining our biological existence. Virtually every time we eat we alert ourselves to God, the Creator of the universe; God, the sustainer of our lives. Religious sensitivity and awe are linked to the human rhythm of eating.

But Jewish tradition goes beyond this. The Torah lists what animals are permissible to be eaten, and which are forbidden. The laws of kashruth clearly delineate two categories of foods: the permitted and the forbidden. Among the forbidden are animals which do not chew their cud nor have split hooves; fish without fins and scales; foods prepared of a mixture of meat and milk. Moreover, even permitted animals may not be eaten unless properly slaughtered according to

Jewish law. The laws of kashruth are quite extensive and play a significant role in the lives of religious Jews.

We may not put any food into our mouths without first knowing that it is kosher. This is an impressive reality. It involves a constant consciousness of the ingredients of the food we buy, of the food served to us; it entails knowledge of the sources of any meat or fish which we eat; it involves keeping our kitchens in such a way that meat and milk items are kept separate. There is perhaps no other such comprehensive regimen in the daily life of the religious Jew.

In terms of the pleasure of food, Jewish tradition has recognized the role of food in generating happiness and good feelings. A Talmudic statement teaches that "there is no happiness except with meat and wine." Shabbat and festivals are to be celebrated with festive meals. The Talmudic sage, Shammai, was said to have set the proper example by buying the best food he could find in the market for his Shabbat meals. If he bought the best food one day, and on the next day found something better, he would buy the better merchandise for Shabbat and eat his first purchase on a weekday. The very celebration of eating is considered a fulfillment of God's commandment to enjoy the holy days.

The symbols surrounding eating reflect the sanctity associated with this basic human experience. The table upon which one eats is considered symbolically to be as the altar in the Temple in Jerusalem. It is consecrated. One is not supposed to treat a table with disrespect, to sit on it, to place one's shoes on it. Before eating a meal, we ritually wash our hands as a sign of purification. Just as Jews entering the Temple in ancient Jerusalem had to purify themselves before coming to the altar, so we must do likewise. We recite the blessing over bread, but before eating it we dip it in salt. This is reminiscent of the practice in the Temple to add salt to the sacrifices offered on the altar.

Sephardim introduce the grace after meals (when at least

three have eaten together) with a verse which states that "this is the table which is before the Lord." This is a further reminder of the sanctity of the table and of the reverence we are supposed to have when eating.

The Menstrual Cycle

Women experience a monthly biological rhythm. From the age of puberty until menopause, women are physically and emotionally involved in this rhythm. The menstrual cycle is governed by an inner "clock"; women experience this connection with the passage of time and the rhythm of physical life in a more direct way than men.

The Torah has taught that a woman is considered ritually impure during her menstrual period. Sexual relations with her husband are forbidden during this time of the month. The practice adopted in Talmudic times has been for women to wait seven clean days following their period. Then they go to a mikveh, a ritual bath, to immerse themselves. Only after the ritual ablution may they resume normal marital relations with their husbands. At the time of the immersion, a blessing is recited acknowledging that God has commanded this form of purification.

Since the menstrual cycle is such a basic feature of a woman's life, and since it recurs regularly at fairly short intervals, it is only to be expected that Jewish religiosity is connected to it. It is part of the mystery of the life process, part of the rhythm of life. A woman during her period becomes separated in certain ways from her normal pattern of life. Her awareness of her bodily functions intensifies. Her recognition of God as Creator should be heightened. Once she has finished her period and waited the seven days following, she immerses in the mikveh. Symbolically, she emerges from the natural water as a new born child, with a sense of awe and amazement. The mikveh experience is a renewal for those who observe it properly. It significantly deepens one's connection with a natural life rhythm and with the God Who created this rhythm.

The Miracle of the Daily Rhythms of Life

The *Amidah*, the silent prayer which is recited three times daily, includes a paragraph of thanksgiving to God. It praises God "for our lives entrusted to Your hand, for our souls in Your care, for Your wonders ever with us, and for Your marvelous goodness towards us at all times, morning, noon and night." Religious rituals deepen our awareness of the providence of God and of our continuous relationship with Him.

The rhythms of daily life are not taken for granted. From our waking and sleeping, to ridding our wastes, to dressing, and to eating—all are windows to a greater awareness of God. Jewish spirituality is intimately connected with these daily rhythms and cannot be divorced from them. We strive always to place God before us, to know Him in all our ways.

6. HALAKHAH, THE JEWISH WAY OF LIFE

Jewish religious tradition provides symbols and observances to bring one into as full an awareness of God's presence as possible. The natural world unfolds the glory of God the Creator; but one can grow accustomed to the phenomena of nature and take them for granted much of the time. Halakhah, Jewish law, adds a dimension of specificity to Jewish spirituality. It is not merely a poetic, artistic experience; it also involves specific activities to do and not to do. The halakhah, which literally means "the way to walk," is a full system and guide for life; through its precepts, the Jew finds himself in a continuous relationship with God.

Halakhah can be understood as the way God wants the people of Israel to conduct their lives. The specific laws, customs and traditions of the Jews must be seen in the context of this definition. If one studies or observes the details of halakhah without full awareness of its divine source, one misses its real meaning.

How do we know God's will, what He wants the people of Israel to do? We know from God's own revealed words, the Torah. The written Torah was accompanied by an oral law, "Torah shebe 'al peh." The original oral law provided explanations and clarifications of the Torah; it also provided the basis for future interpretation of the Torah by the rabbinic authorities of the Great Court.[1]

One category of the oral Torah includes explanations of

the Torah which were given by God to Moses. For example, in Leviticus 23:40 the Torah commands in regard to Succoth: "And you shall take on the first day the fruit of a beautiful tree, branches of palm trees, and boughs of thick trees and willows of the brook and you shall rejoice before the Lord your God seven days." The verse does not specify which fruit from a beautiful tree should be taken! Nor does it give the specifications for the other items to be taken either—how many palm branches, how many boughs, in what condition, for how long etc.? Yet, Moses must have received instruction from God concerning these details, since it was his job to teach the law to the people of Israel. Therefore, we must conclude that God conveyed to Moses the necessary information. For example, the "fruit of the beautiful tree" is an *ethrog* (citron); when we take an *ethrog* on Succoth we are fulfilling the will of God as expressed in this commandment both through the written and oral Torah.

Another example is from Deuteronomy 6:8, where we learn that the words of the Torah are to be bound "as a sign upon your hand and as frontlets between your eyes." But how is this verse to be understood? Since the language is vague and open to interpretation, Moses must have received clarification from God originally. The oral law explains this verse to be referring to *tefillin* and provides the details: *tefillin* must be made of leather, must be black, must include certain Biblical passages.

The oral interpretations of the Torah are intrinsic to the understanding of the written Torah. Indeed, they are also expressions of God's will. Halakhah in its pure sense, then, goes directly back to the word of God as expressed in the Torah and in the oral explanations of the Torah given to Moses.

The words of the Torah, even with their ancient explanations, still leave many questions unanswered. The language of the Torah is not legalistic, for the most part. Even in its legalistic sections, it is not usually precise as a code of law.

The words of the Torah demand explanation and interpretation. The Torah provides us with the word of God—but also leaves much room for human interpretation and application of principles. Due to changed conditions and/or perceptions, the words of the Torah are not always easily applied to contemporary life. Therefore, the halakhah also includes categories of rabbinic law. The rabbis of each generation are given the responsibility and authority to apply the teachings of the Torah to their own situation. Categories of rabbinic law include a) laws derived by hermeneutic principles, by interpretations of the Torah; b) rabbinical ordinances; c) local regulations and customs.

These categories of halakhah are not based directly on God's command, but on the rabbinic application of Torah principles to their contemporary situations. The Torah and the original oral law represent God's words to Israel; the rabbinic categories of halakhah represent the effort of human beings to derive God's will from the principles of the Torah.

The Great Court In Jerusalem

Since Jewish life is entirely involved in halakhah, it is necessary for Jews to know exactly what the halakhah requires of them. The role of rabbis and teachers has always been to elucidate the halakhah, to deal with practical and theoretical halakhic questions brought to them by interested Jews.

In ancient Israel, there was a great court in Jerusalem— popularly known as the Sanhedrin—which was the recognized authoritative body to pronounce the halakhah. Whenever a controversy arose involving Jewish law in Israel, local rabbinic courts would pass judgement to resolve it. When the controversy was too difficult to handle on the local level, it was brought before the Great Court in Jerusalem and was solved there. There was no further recourse. The decision of the Great Court was authoritative.

The Great Court not only responded to problems brought

to it, but also devoted itself to studying the Torah and establishing how the Torah laws should be applied. The Great Court performed judicial and legislative functions.

Moses Maimonides, in his classic code of halakhah, describes the Great Court in the following terms (Laws of Rebels 1:1): "The Great Court in Jerusalem represents the essence of the oral Torah. Its members are the pillars of direction; law and order emanate from them to all of Israel. And upon them the Torah rests its trust, as it says: 'You shall act in accordance with the directions they give you' (Deuteronomy 17:11). This is a positive commandment; anyone who believes in Moses our teacher and in his Torah is obligated to rely upon them in matters of religion and to depend on them." The Great Court in Jerusalem, then, was the institution which preserved and developed all aspects of the oral law. It maintained the ancient traditions going back to Moses, and also added its own interpretations, ordinances and customs in order to guide the lives of the Israelites.

The Great Court had the authority to interpret the Torah and to declare its judgement concerning the will of God. Yet, interpretations could change from one generation to the next; the oral law was "oral" so that it would retain fluidity and flexibility. Maimonides writes (Laws of Rebels 2:1): "A Great Court which interpreted scripture using one of the principles of interpretation, and ruled according to the way it seemed to them that the law should be—their judgement is the law. If a subsequent Great Court found a reason to refute their decision, it should refute it and judge according to the way it seems to them, as it says 'to the judge who will be in those days,'—you are only obligated to follow the Court which is in your generation."

Under certain circumstances, the Great Court even had the power to overrule a law of the Torah (see for example the discussion in the Talmud, Yebamot 90b). Each Court had the right and responsibility to use its own understanding in applying the word of God to the life of the people of Israel.

When the Great Court of Jerusalem ceased to operate and the Jews were exiled by the Romans (c. 68 C.E.), a group of rabbis attempted to re-establish authority in a rabbinical court in Yavneh. The effort was important, but short-lived. After the Bar Kokhba rebellion (135 C.E.), many of the leading sages were executed by the Romans, and the establishment of a central authoritative rabbinic court proved unfeasible. Rabbi Yehudah the Prince, in the mid-second century C.E., compiled the Mishnah, a record of the oral law up to his time. From then on, the Mishnah became the central text in hala-khah; rabbis no longer derived laws directly from the text of the Torah, but focussed their studies and decisions on the text of the Mishnah. Rabbinical discussions of the Mishnah became knows as the Gemara; the Mishnah and Gemara to-gether are known as the Talmud. The Talmud became the base of all halakhic discussions and decisions.

Over the generations, many other layers of rabbinic scholarship have been added to halakhic literature. In gen-eral terms, these include the writings of the *Geonim* (scholars of Babylonia, 6th through 10th centuries); *Rishonim* (11th through 15th centuries); *Aharonim* (16th through 19th cen-turies); as well as of modern contemporary sages.

The dissolution of the Great Court changed the method of halakhah. No longer was there one universally recognized institution which could rule authoritatively for all Jews. No longer did rabbis go directly to the Torah in order to de-termine halakhah. Instead of having an oral law which could be somewhat fluid, halakhah became based on written texts and was dependent on precedents. For example, no rabbi of any reputation today will write a responsum without quoting earlier authorities and the Talmud before presenting his own decision. Seldom will the Torah itself be cited to prove a point of law.

A Modern Sanhedrin?

As has been seen, the process of the halakhah underwent a significant change with the loss of the Great Court. Rabbis and laymen have not had a central religious body to resolve their dilemmas. Amazingly, Jews have flourished for nearly two thousand years in many different lands without having a basic institution of halakhah. In spite of differences of custom and emphasis which have arisen among different groups of Jews, the essential unity of halakhah was preserved. To this day, every Jew who adheres to halakhah shares in a truly remarkable historic, religious, sociological, spiritual and national enterprise.

There have been some individuals who have called for the establishment of a new Sanhedrin in our times. They would like a revival of a central halakhic authority for the Jewish people. The Sanhedrin would not only provide unity in halakhah, but would re-institute the original methodology of the oral law—interpreting the Torah itself, applying the law to life with the freedom to overrule precedents and previous decisions.

One of those calling for a Sanhedrin was the Sephardic Chief Rabbi of Israel, Rabbi Benzion Uziel (1880-1953). In a speech delivered on 12 Kislev 5697, he called for an authoritative rabbinic body along the lines of the Great Court of Jerusalem.[2] He viewed this effort as a continuation of the work of Rabbi Yohanan ben Zaccai, who had been instrumental in establishing a quasi-Sanhedrin in Yavneh following the destruction of Jerusalem by the Romans.

Rabbi Uziel believed it was the responsibility of the rabbinate to work to achieve this goal. Rabbis are delegated the responsibility of establishing *mishpat*, justice. This refers not only to cases between contending individuals, but also to public issues, questions of taxation and communal needs. By working for a Sanhedrin, the rabbis will be working for a unifying force in Jewish life. Rabbi Uziel argued that one who simply knew how to rule on what is permitted and what is forbidden, or on who is guilty and who is innocent—such a person is not truly in the category of being a *posek*, a decisor of halakhah. This person is known as a *talmid* or *talmid haham*, a student or a wise student. To be a *posek*, however, involves having the power of the Great Court. Only the Sanhedrin can serve as a real *posek*. "The responsibility of the Sanhedrin was to clarify and distinguish between true interpretations (which are true to the spirit of the Torah) and casuistic interpretations (which are erroneous)."[3]

Rabbi Uziel writes that the *posek* draws conclusions from the Torah and the words of the prophets, as well as from the traditional oral law. "The *posek* in Israel is not bound by precedents of the *posek* of laws who precedes him. If he was, this would lead to great damage, in that an accidental error would be fixed as a permanent halakhah even though it was erroneous in its foundation. In order to avoid this harmful eventuality, the authority of the Great Court was restricted only to the time in which it sits on the chair of judgement. But the decisions of the Great Court are not established as law and do not obligate the judges who will come after them to judge and to teach like them."[4]

Rabbi Uziel was deeply impressed by the work of Moses Maimonides and believed that he deserved the title *posek*. Maimonides worked to make the laws of the Torah known to the general public. In his comprehensive code of Jewish law, Maimonides recorded the halakhah anonymously to signify that it represents a concensus, not just the opinion of individuals. He not only gathered his material from all rabbinic literature, but he also derived benefit from the teachings of non-Jewish thinkers. "In this matter, by the way, Maimonides has informed us that in halakhic decisions one must comprehend all things on the basis of their content and truth, and not on the authority of their authors alone. Maimonides taught a great principle: Accept the truth from those who have stated it."[5]

In order to restore a central authority for halakhah, Rabbi Uziel urged: "Let us arise and establish the Great Court in Jerusalem, not in order to judge cases of fines, or capital cases, and not in order to permit the firstborn because of its blemish. Rather, let us do so in order to solve the questions of life which confront us each day in our settlements and in our world; and in order to create a beginning for our destined redemption: 'And I will return your judges as in the beginning and your advisers as formerly; for out of Zion will the Torah proceed and the word of God from Jerusalem.' "[6]

Until a Great Court is re-established in Jerusalem, the halakhah is taught by leading rabbinical sages who draw on the vast rabbinic literature which has developed over the past several thousand years. There are variations of opinion on details of halakhah; different sages rule differently: yet, the halakhic process continues to provide the framework for religious Jewish life. In order for a sage to be recognized as authoritative, he must not only have great erudition; he must not only be personally observant of halakhah; he must also be fully faithful to the idea that halakhah is the expression of the will of God to the Jewish people. Halakhah, therefore, must be taken seriously on its own terms.

A Sephardic Approach To Halakhah[7]

Without a Great Court in Jerusalem, it was only natural that different approaches to halakhah developed among various Jewish communities during the past nearly two thousand years. Customs and practices varied from place to place and from time to time. Attitudes towards halakhic study also differed. Certainly, the basic assumptions of the divinity of the Torah and the authority of halakhah were accepted: but differences in style definitely did exist among religious Jewish communities throughout the ages.

Two major streams of Jewish tradition are the Ashkenazic and the Sepahardic. Ashkenizim (Ashkenaz means Germany in Hebrew) primarily lived in Europe. In the Middle

Ages they were concentrated in France, Germany and Italy; gradually, the centers of Ashkenazic Jewry shifted to Poland, Russia and Eastern Europe in general. The common feature of these communities is that they existed in Christian countries. They were included within the orbit of Western civilization.

The Westernization of these communities was intensified during the eighteenth and nineteenth centuries—when European Jews were gaining rights of citizenship in the countries in which they lived. The doors of Western civilization opened to them as never before; Jews studied in European universities, advanced in professional, cultural and political life. Their struggles for civil rights were painful and not fully successful. Anti-Jewish attitudes and actual violence against Jews ultimately led many Ashkenazim to migrate to Israel, the United States and other safe havens. The Nazi holocaust during World War II decimated European Jewry, most of which was of Ashkenazic background. Yet, Ashkenazic Jewry today represents a large majority of world Jewry.

Ashkenazic numerical dominance has been matched by its cultural hegemony as well. Certainly, for the past three centuries and more, Ashkenazic rabbis have dominated halakhah; Ashkenazic thinkers have dominated Jewish philosophy; Ashkenazic writers and artists have dominated Jewish cultural life.

The Sephardic Jews (Sepharad refers to Spain in Hebrew) enjoyed their period of dominance during the centuries prior to the expulsion of Jews from Spain in 1492. The contributions of Sephardim to all areas of Jewish scholarship and thought as well as to science, medicine, and mathematics were impressive, unequalled in the Jewish world. Even during the century following the expulsion, Sephardic Jewry maintained a dynamic spiritual and cultural life which influenced world Jewry.

The considerable majority of Sephardim who left the Iberian Peninsula settled in Moslem countries. Although Sephardim also went to Italy, Holland, France and other Western European locations, the much greater number flourished in non-Western environments. The Ottoman Empire provided haven for Sephardic refugees. Sephardic communities developed throughout Turkey, the Balkan countries, the Middle East and North Africa. Their experience was different in many ways from that of the Ashkenazim of Europe. Indeed, the two groups of Jews—those of Christian Europe and those of the Moslem domains—lived in relative isolation one from the other.

Although it is difficult to generalize about differences in the realm of halakhah, it may be argued that there were different trends of halakhic thinking among the two groups, just as there were differences in world views in general. It is of interest to explore the Sephardic approach to halakhah since it may serve as an anodyne to the prevailing Ashkenazic approach. Since Sephardim lived among non-Western people, their perceptions and attitudes about Judaism may serve as a counter-balance to the preponderant Westernization of Judaism.

A people's attitudes are often conveyed through their words and actions when they are not self-conscious about being observed. They are implied in proverbs and songs, in the way people dress, in their gestures, in the way they express themselves. In order to comprehend a Sephardic approach to halakhah, one must attempt to grasp the un-documented, non-explicit elements of Sephardic culture— elements which are known from sharing a people's mentality.

One element which needs to be considered is joie de vivre. While Sephardim living in Moslem lands over the past four centuries were generally quite observant of halakhah, their observance did not lead them to become somber or overly serious. Pious Sephardim sang Judeo-Spanish love ballads and drinking songs at family celebrations in a natural way, without self-consciousness. Singing in a lighthearted spirit, even at public gatherings, did not strike them as being irreverent. Rather, the pleasures and aesthetics of this world were viewed in a positive light.

Sephardic holiday celebrations and life cycle observances, for example, were characterized by the preparation of elaborate delicacies to eat, the singing of songs, and a general spirit of gaiety and hospitality. Sephardim appreciated colorful fabrics, fine embroidery, excellent craftsmanship in metals. On every happy occasion there was bound to be the fragrance of rose water, herbs, fresh fruits. All of these accoutrements—song, food, fragrances, decorative materials—gave the specific religious observance its distinctive quality. These things were not peripheral to halakhah, but gave halakhah its proper context: a context of love, happiness, optimism.

This spirit carried itself even to the serious season of the High Holy Days, when self-scrutiny and repentance were expected. The travel account of Rabbi Simhah ben Joshua of Zalozhtsy (1711-1768) sheds interesting light on this fact.[8] He travelled to the Holy Land with a group of ascetic Hassidim in 1764, and the majority of his Jewish co-passengers on the ship were Sephardim. The rabbi noted that "the Sephardim awoke before daybreak to say penitential prayers in a congregation, as is their custom in the month of Elul." He then added: "During the day they eat and rejoice and are happy at heart." For Rabbi Simhah, this behavior seemed paradoxical; but the Sephardim themselves did not even realize that their behavior was in any way noteworthy. Their unstated assumption was that eating, rejoicing and being happy of heart were not in conflict with piety, even in the serious season of penitential prayers.

Alan Watts has pointed out that in Western thought the individual is "split." He is both himself and an observer of himself. Western culture teaches us to analyze ourselves, to see ourselves as though we are somehow outside of ourselves. We are both subjects and objects. Carried to an extreme, this way of viewing ourselves can be confusing and guilt-inducing—it is as though we live our lives while seeing ourselves in a mirror. We are apt to become overly self-conscious, self-critical, and self-centered. Eastern culture, on the other hand, tends to be more holistic, less self-analytic. People are taught to live naturally and easily, without objectifying themselves overly much.

Watts has written: "The most spiritual people are the most human. They are natural and easy in manner; they give themselves no airs; they interest themselves in ordinary everyday matters, and are not forever talking and thinking *about* religion. For them there is no difference between spirituality and usual life, and to their awakened insight the lives of the most humdrum and earth-bound people are as much in harmony with the infinite as their own."[9]

The Sephardim tended to have the Eastern, rather than the Western, attitude on life. The halakhah was observed naturally and easily, as a vital part of life. Andre Chouraqui, in his study of North African Jewry, has noted that the Jews of the Maghreb were quite observant of halakhah; and "the Judaism of the most conservative of the Maghreb's Jews was marked by a flexibility, a hospitality, a tolerance . . ." The Jews of North Africa had a "touching generosity of spirit and a profound respect for meditation."[10] These comments are equally applicable to Sephardim throughout the Mediterranean area. To borrow from the terminology of geometry, the Ashkenazim tended to prefer sharp angles while Sephardim tended to prefer circles and rounded edges.

This analogy was placed in halakhic terms by Rabbi Hayyim Yosef David Azulai (1724-1806), one of the leading rabbinic figures of his time. He wrote that in matters of halakhah, Sephardic sages clung to the quality of *hesed*, kindness, and tended to be lenient. Ashkenazim manifested the quality of *geburah*, heroism, and therefore tended to be strict. Azulai's statement—regardless of its objective truth— is a profound indication of his own self-image. He and nu-

merous other Sephardic rabbis saw themselves as agents of
hesed. This self-image could not but influence the manner in
which they dealt with questions of halakhah. *Hesed* was not
merely a pleasant idea but a working principle.

H. J. Zimmels, in his book "Ashkenazim and Sephardim," indicates that as a general rule Sephardim were more
lenient than the Ashkenazim in their halakhic rulings.[11] He
suggests that the Ashkenazic inclination to stringency was
largely the result of centuries of persecution suffered by
German Jewry. It also stemmed from the doctrines of the
German Hassidim of the 12th and 13th centuries, who emphasized strictness in religious observance. Groups of Ashkenazic Jews imposed upon themselves greater stringencies
than the law demanded and, in time, many of these observances became normative.

Rabbi Benzion Uziel offered an insight into the differences between Sephardic and Ashkenazic sages. Sephardic
rabbis felt powerful enough in their opinion and authority to
annul customs which were not based on halakhic foundations. In contrast, Ashkenazic rabbis tended to strengthen
customs and sought support for them even if they seemed
strange or without halakhic basis. The rabbis of France and
Germany had a negative opinion of the rabbis of Spain, feeling that the Sephardic sages were too independent and irreverent to tradition. On the other hand, the Sephardim felt
that their method was correct and were quite proud of pro-
moting it.[12]

Sephardic tradition stressed the idea that the halakhah is
a practical guide to behavior. It is not a metaphysical system
set aside for an intellectual elite. On the contrary, each person
was entitled and obligated to understand what the halakhah
requires. It is not surprising, therefore, that the classic codes
of Jewish law were produced in Sephardic communities.
Sephardic scholars studied texts with the goal of applying
their rules directly to actual situations; therefore, they had to

remain sensitive to the needs of people. This very sensitivity helped maintain the quality of hesed in halakhah.

When halakhah is studied as an intellectual system divorced from actual life situations, it may follow the dictates of logic and intricate reasoning rather than the dictates of human kindness. A legal conclusion might be reached in the abstract and then be applied to human conditions as a derrick operation from above. This approach is contrary to the overall spirit of Sephardic halakhic thought.

Although it is incumbent upon each Jew to study Torah and halakhah, difficult questions and disputes cannot always be solved by the individuals involved. Thus, over the past centuries, Sephardic communities normally appointed a chief rabbi, often referred to as "haham," sage. He had the final word in matters of halakhah for his community. The institution of haham provided the Jews with a recognized authority who could resolve their questions. When the Sephardim of the Island of Rhodes wanted to appoint a chief rabbi in the early 17th century, they agreed that no one had the right to contest the haham's rulings. "All which he will decide will be correct and acceptable as the law which was determined by the Court of Rabban Gamliel. . . . All which he will decide . . . will be correct and acceptable as a law of God's Torah as it was given at Sinai."[13]

The Jews of Rhodes linked their haham's authority to that of the powerful court of Rabban Gamliel and to the Torah itself. Other Sephardic communties did likewise. This was a way of restoring, at least on a communal level, the original function of the Great Court in Jerusalem, which, according to Maimonides, was the essential institution of the halakhah. Rabbi Joseph Taitasak (16th century, Salonika) expressed this idea clearly: "Know that each and every community has authority over its members, for every community may legislate in its city just as the Great Court could legislate for all Israel."[14]

Law and Life

Since halakhah is an all-encompassing guide to life which describes what God wants us to do, it is essential that we understand its role in our lives. Observing the mitzvot is a Jew's way of connecting himself with the eternal reality of God. To treat halakhah as a mechanical system of laws is to miss its meaning and significance. Halakhah provides the framework for spiritual awareness, religious insight, and even spontaneity.

At the root of halakhah is the awareness that God is overwhelmingly great and that human beings are over-whelmingly limited. Humility is the hallmark of the truly religious person. One must open himself to the spirit of God which flows through the halakhah, and must give himself to the religious experience.

A true sage must be humble; arrogance is a sign of not understanding the real lesson of halakhah. Solomon Schechter, in his beautiful essay about the mystics of Safed of the 16th century, quotes Shlomel of Moravia who described the scholars, saints and men of good deeds of Safed, indicating that many of them were worthy of receiving the Divine Spirit. "None among them is ashamed to go to the well and draw water and carry home the pitcher on his shoulders, or go to the market to buy bread, oil and vegetables. All the work in the house is done by themselves."[15] These sages followed the model of Talmudic rabbis who also did not find it beneath their dignity to work at menial tasks. Egotism and a sense of inflated self-importance are contrary to the spirit of Jewish religiosity.

It is interesting to note how this ideal has been somewhat diminished among Western Jews. Isidore Epstein, in his study of the responsa of Rabbi Simon Duran, displays a Western bias when he writes that "the multifarious functions of the rabbis [of North Africa] also testify to the low standards of Jewish culture of North African Jewry. In adverting to

Jewish past and present day history, we cannot fail to notice that wherever there is a strong, virile and advanced Jewish life, there is the tendency to keep the rabbinical office distinct from other callings; and the combination of rabbinical charges with other functions is a sign of decadence and of lack of appreciation of learning as such. North Africa in our period exhibited that characteristic system of cultural decline. There the rabbi was not "rabbi" in the understood sense of the word, but combined with that office the functions of school teacher, slaughterer, and reader to the consequent lowering in his prestige and rabbinical authority."[16] Epstein's assumption that it is a sign of decadence when rabbis assume responsibilities other than purely academic is quite absurd. The contrary seems much truer. The Talmudic sages assumed other responsibilities as did the outstanding sages of the Sephardic world; and they did not feel demeaned thereby. It is precisely when rabbis relegate to themselves purely academic functions and when they consider it undignified to meet other communal needs that egotism and pettiness arise. It is actually to the credit of North African Jews and many other Sephardic communities as well, that rabbis often served in practical capacities, participating more fully in the life of their communities. This was not at all a shame for them or a reflection of cultural decadence for the communities.

Humility is a virtue which halakhah fosters for sages and laymen alike. Rabbi David Ibn Zimra (16th century) offered an explanation of a rabbinic dictum that one is not supposed to argue with the greatest of the judges who has made a ruling on a legal question. Yet, what if he is wrong? Shouldn't the lesser judges have the right and responsibility to dissent? Rabbi David Ibn Zimra explains that the dictum was not intended as a warning for the lesser judges but rather for the greatest judge. The judge occupying the highest position should not give his decision first because others will be afraid to argue with him. His decision will intimidate the others.

Therefore, true justice demands that the greater judges withhold their opinions until the lesser ones have had their say. In this way, all opinions can be evaluated fairly, without intimidation or arrogance.[17]

In a similar spirit, Rabbi Hayyim Yosef David Azulai comments on a passage in the Ethics of the Fathers which says that each person should prepare himself to study Torah since it does not come to him as an inheritance. Rabbi Azulai notes that each sage received his specific portion from Sinai and therefore even a great sage needs to learn from others. No scholar is self-sufficient, no sage inherits all wisdom. It is necessary for everyone to be humble, to be open to the opinions of others, to try to learn from everyone.[18]

Piety

Many wonderful and horrible things have been done in the name of religion. George Bernard Shaw once wrote: "Beware of a man whose God is in Heaven." It is difficult, perhaps impossible, to have reasonable communication with someone who feels that he knows Truth, that only he and those who share his beliefs are absolutely right.

There have been great prophets, mystics and pietists who have lived their lives in relationship with God. There have also been inquisitors, murderers and arrogant criminals who have thought that they acted according to the will of God. If religion attracts the most sensitive and thoughtful people, it also draws those who wish to seem important and holy in the eyes of others, who use the cloak of religion to hide their own egocentric purposes.

Since the Jewish religious tradition is deeply tied to halakhah, it is not surprising that there have been people who have found their self-importance in legalism. There is a fine line between pious devotion and misguided asceticism. Rabbi Hayyim Yosef David Azulai has taught that one should not follow unnecessary stringencies in law. Even in private, one should not be overly stringent, unless he is motivated by pure and humble piety.[19] Those who do accept additional obligations upon themselves should not consider themselves superior to others who do not accept such stringencies. A truly pious person feels no need to compare his piety to that of others; his life is lived in relationship to God; he lives with humility and equanimity.

Jewish history has witnessed the honest spirituality of innumerable pious men and women who have sincerely served God through their observance of halakhah. It has also witnessed pietistic movements, where groups of people observed Jewish law with intensity and introduced pious customs into Jewish religious life. Such movements include the German Hassidim of the 13th century; the Sephardic mystical schools of the 16th century; the Hassidic movement of the 17th century; the Musar movement of the 19th century. These and other religious movements called on Jews to deepen their religious experience by intensifying their observance of halakhah and by adopting additional pious practices.

Rabbi Mosheh Cordovero of 16th century Safed, for example, composed a list of rules for Jews to observe. The following are some of his recommendations.[20]

One should not turn his heart from meditating on Torah and holiness, so that his heart will constantly be a sanctuary for the Divine Presence. He should never allow himself to become angry. One should always be concerned about the needs of his fellow beings and should behave kindly to them. One should behave nicely, even with those who transgress the laws of the Torah.

One should not drink wine except on Shabbat and holy days. He should pray with concentration. He should not speak badly about any person or any other living creation of God. He should never speak falsehood or even imply falsehood. One should meet with a friend each Friday evening to review what has occurred during the course of the past week.

One should recite the afternoon prayer with a prayer shawl and tefillin. He should chant the Grace after Meals aloud. Each night he should sit on the ground and lament the destruction of the Temple in Jerusalem; he should also cry over his own sins which lengthen the time before our ultimate redemption.

A person should avoid being part of four groups which do not receive the Divine Presence: hypocrites, liars, idlers and those who speak evil about others. One should give charity each day in order to atone for his sins. One should pay his pledges immediately and not postpone them. One should confess his sins prior to eating and prior to going to sleep. A person should fast as often as his health allows.

These rules, and other similar ones, stem from the overwhelming desire of religiously sensitive people to serve God in fullness. The more they can do, the closer they feel to the Almighty. When their deeds are observed in the spirit of love and selflessness, they are spiritually meaningful. The problem, of course, is that these rules of piety may themselves become merely mechanical observances.

The genius of halakhah is that it provides Jews with a medium for approaching God on a constant basis. Each law, each observance is a link between the human and the Divine. But the power of halakhah cannot be appreciated without spiritual sensitivity, openness and—above all—humility.

Saintliness

It is a rare experience to be in the presence of a truly saintly person, one who lives his/her life in a deep relationship with God. We might describe such a person as having wisdom, humility, inner peace, tranquility. The saintly person lives life on a different plane from most other people.

One cannot attain saintliness as the result of following any specific prescriptions. There are no schools to educate and graduate saints. There are no rituals or techniques which, if followed, will result automatically in the creation of a genuinely pious person.

In describing the actions and observances of deeply pious people, we only describe the evident and superficial aspect of their lives. Their inner lives remain a secret to us. We are intrigued with such people because we do not understand their inner beings.

Following the external dictates of halakhah does not guarantee the quality of saintliness. Without mystical insight, without an all-encompassing love, the practitioner of halakhah mimics saintliness. Halakhah must be experienced as a fulfillment of the will of God if it is to generate spirituality.

Modern Western society does not place a particularly high premium on saintliness. Our society is achievement-oriented, pragmatic, material-centered. Even religion is profoundly influenced by these values. Religious institutions are concerned with perpetuating themselves—raising money, obtaining members, providing services. Prayer services might pass for good (or not so good) theater. They may provide parodies of prayer, where people appear to be praying while having no sense of the presence of God. It is difficult to preach about God and mystical saintliness except to unusual individuals.

The ideal of halakhah is to create *tsaddikim*, righteous people. Even those who may never attain this spiritual level still need to know what the goal is.

In describing the religious life of North African Jewry, Andre Chouraqui has noted that the Jews of the Maghreb valued saintliness as the ultimate quality.[21] They expected that their rabbis be well-versed in Torah and rabbinic literature; but more than this, they expected them to be able to pray with sincerity and real devotion. By being in the presence of saintly teachers, the average people could be raised in their own spiritual life.

In a society which values saintliness as the ultimate human goal, it is more natural to achieve piety. It is far more difficult to attain saintliness in a pragmatic, materialistic culture, unless one divorces himself from the culture in which he lives.

In summation, halakhah is the ever-present link between God and the Jewish people. Through observance of halakhah in the spirit of humility, the Jew has the opportunity to live his life on a deep, spiritual level. The goal of halakhah is to create righteous, saintly people.

7. | REVELATION

God reveals Himself as Creator, through the world which He has created and which He maintains. A thoughtful human being may see in the natural phenomena a reflection of God. Jewish tradition ties the Jew to the rhythms of nature in order to deepen one's experience of God the Creator.

God has also revealed Himself to the people of Israel at Mount Sinai. The Torah and halakhah are reflections of the will of God. By studying the Torah and observing the halakhah, the religious Jew has a unique path to God. As has been noted in the previous chapter, the observance of halakhah is meaningful insofar as it is understood to be a fulfillment of God's will. Since halakhah is an all-embracing system of life which governs virtually every instant of life, the pious Jew has the opportunity of reaching great spiritual heights and maintaining an almost constant relationship with God.

God's revelation through nature may be experienced by all people, Jews and non-Jews alike. But nature leads us to an awe and love for the Creator while not giving us any insight as to how to conduct our lives according to His will. The revelation through Torah comes to fill this void, to give specific direction to the Jewish people as to how they should live within a special relationship to God.

Maimonides, in his "Guide for the Perplexed" (Part 3, Chapter 51), has explained that "such religious acts as studying the Torah, praying, and the performance of other precepts, serve exclusively as the means of causing us to occupy and fill our mind with the precepts of God, and free it from worldly business; for we are thus, as it were, in communication with God, and undisturbed by any other thing."

So both nature and the Torah provide paths to God. The "communication" which God sends to humans, though, is dependent on a person's sensitivity to "hear" the message. It is possible for different people to experience the same phenomenon and have entirely different reactions. In other words, it is not just a matter of observing an objective reality, but also of experiencing it subjectively.

Yet, the history of religion also records many examples of individuals who have communed with God not merely by being sensitive to nature and sacred texts; but who have claimed actually to have heard God's voice. In these communications, the originator is God and He communicates with words. Such communications are in the category of direct revelations of God. They are claimed to be objectively true, not simply subjectively meaningful experiences.

How are we to understand such revelations? It is difficult to explain in logical, reasonable terms that the eternal and infinite God speaks with words to mortal humans. Revelation cannot be proven or demonstrated by philosophy or theology, but only by first-hand experience. Yehudah Halevy argued in his "Kuzari" that the genuineness of God's revelation to the Israelites at Sinai is proven by the experience of the Israelites themselves. Hundreds of thousands of them literally heard the voice of God. This was a primary, objective event that could not be denied or explained away. We can trust in the truth of that revelation since so many of our ancestors were first-hand participants in it. The historical record of the primary event has been passed down through all the generations.

It is one thing to study the revelation; and another to actually experience it. We need to understand more about the primary experience of direct revelation.

The Torah is filled with the sound of the voice of God. He speaks to Biblical characters, gives them messages and commandments. God talks to the Biblical heroes and they respond in a natural way, as though it is quite normal to carry on a conversation with God. Biblical characters seldom express amazement at having received divine communications.

Abraham and Sarah are old. They feel the deep pain of Sarah's barrenness. Angels appear and tell the couple that they will have a son. The child, Isaac, is born. Some years pass, and Abraham hears a voice: "Take your son, your only son, whom you love, Isaac, and go to the land of Moriah, and offer him there for a burnt offering on one of the mountains which I will tell you of." The message is shocking and terrible, but Abraham offers no words in response. He wakes up early the next morning, takes his son, and leaves on this mysterious journey to an undesignated mountain. Abraham did not doubt that the voice he heard was God's. He was so certain of the reality of God's communication that he was prepared to take the life of his son.

Moses is a shepherd in Midian. One day, as he is tending his flock, he spots a burning bush. The flames rise but the bush is not consumed. A voice calls out to Moses, tells him to return to Egypt to lead the Israelites to freedom. Moses feels inadequate to the task; yet, the voice insists. Moses leaves the tranquility of his life in Midian and goes to Egypt to redeem the children of Israel. Moses never wondered whether the voice was God or simply his own imagination. Having heard the voice, Moses knew the truth.

God's revelations to humans are the point of contact between the eternal reality of God and the time-bound reality of humanity. Why it happens, how it happens—no one can explain with certainty. But human experience knows that it has happened and does happen.

Rabbi Benzion Uziel, in an essay dealing with the phenomenon of prophecy, considers the opinions of various philosophers concerning how people are able to hear God's voice. What was the experience of the Israelites at Sinai or the experience of the prophets? Rabbi Uziel believes that the voice of God is heard "through channels of the senses of sight and hearing, the results of the formations of air in the form of letters, seen by the eye, or as a created voice which the God of the universe created and initiated. . . . "[1] In effect, God creates within the human the power to receive His communication; and the communication is not heard in the same way that one hears the words or sounds of other humans.

Medical and psychological research have shown that probing certain parts of the human brain can evoke specific responses. A person might begin to taste, smell, hear, see or feel something, not in response to an outside stimulus but to the probings in his brain. Likewise, the prophetic experience may involve hearing God's words not by means of one's external senses, but by God's implanting the words in a person's brain.

Maimonides believed that prophecy was attained only by those who were worthy of it. But Rabbi Uziel argues that prophecy was experienced and can be experienced by anyone whom God chooses, regardless of qualifications. Rabbi Yosef Albo has written that when a prophet is present, prophecy itself can be spread even to individuals who are not ordinarily fit to receive prophecy, just as was the case at the revelation at Sinai where everyone heard the voice of God. Rabbi Uziel notes that "these words of Rabbi Yosef Albo have a great basis in life, for our eyes see that the presence of a heroic man at the head of his army spreads a spirit of heroism and courage over his troops, even those who are weak in nature and timid in spirit." A prophet has a similar power to spread prophecy over his followers.

The Midrash Tanhuma (Exodus 1:22) describes the voice of God at Sinai as having emerged when the world was in total silence. The voice seemed to come from every direction and then from heaven. Rabbi Uziel interprets this midrash as teaching that the voice of God at Sinai was unique, not emanating from an organic body nor even having a specific place as its source.[2] Rather, it was a miraculous voice which filled the entire universe. The midrash teaches that all the voices on earth have echoes but that the voice of God at Sinai had no echo. It changed into seven voices and into seventy languages and was heard by each individual according to his power. The voice was not heard by the hearing canals, but was somehow absorbed by the entire beings of the Israelites.

Rabbi Uziel continues: "Those enlightened ones err who follow the Greek philosopher who says that anything that cannot be understood by reason is not true. To these hard-hearted and stupid people we say: have you never heard in your life the voice of God which speaks to you in the hiddenness of the soul? A hidden and secret voice which makes all your limbs tremble and shake? And you are moved by it, and you rejoice. from happiness at this voice which guides you and chastises you, which consoles and strengthens, teaches and enlightens, and reveals to you the truth in its clarity in ways which have no evidence in any other way. . . . Whence comes this hidden voice? And how does it reach your ears and your heart?" Hearing this inner voice is an experience found among all people, each according to his own intelligence and sensitivity. This experience can give us an inkling into the revelation at Sinai. Though we cannot understand how the revelation was experienced, we cannot doubt its wondrous truth. "The voice of God heard by our ancestors at the revelation at Sinai returns, and is heard by our ears and our hearts each day through the Torah which goes with us always, to teach us the way of life in which to walk, and to bring us closer under the wings of the holy Shekhinah of the Holy One of Israel."

The experience of revelation is personal and subjective, yet its truth is so clear that it transcends rational and logical limitations. Each individual experiences revelation differently, each according to his powers. This idea has an antecedent in the writings of Rabbi Isaac Luria of 16th century

Safed. Rabbi Luria taught that there are 600,000 aspects of meaning in the Torah, equal to the number of Israelites who witnessed the revelation at Sinai. The Torah in its fullness cannot be understood unless these 600,000 facets are considered. This idea was also expressed by Rabbi Mosheh Cordovero who taught that each of the 600,000 souls has its own special portion of the Torah, "and that to none other than he, whose soul springs from thence, will it be given to understand it in this special and individual way that is reserved to him."[3]

Revelation versus Religion

Judaism is founded on revelation and prophecy. When God spoke the Ten Commandments to the people of Israel at Sinai, He established a covenant for all time. The sacred texts of Judaism record God's words to our ancestors.

But a paradoxical situation arises. Although revelation and prophecy lay at the foundation of our religious tradition, they are also the most potentially dangerous and unsettling elements within religion. Anyone can claim to have heard the voice of God or to have received a vision from the Almighty. History is studded with an array of false prophets. Even in Biblical times it was not easy to distinguish between a genuine prophet and an imposter. Jeremiah debated against false prophets; but he was not believed by many of his coreligionists. Elijah, after having performed a spectacular miracle on Mount Carmel in the presence of a large throng of people, had to flee for his life on the very next day. He prayed to God to allow him to die. Apparently, the Israelites were not completely convinced of his divine mission.

Imagine if a father today held a knife to his son's throat. And suppose the father explained that he must sacrifice his son in response to a commandment he received from God. Surely, we would do all in our power to stop him, perhaps imagining him to be deranged. Yet, Abraham did the same thing in response to the voice he heard, and is judged to be a hero of faith. Who can determine who has actually received a revelation from God and who has not?

Religion, though based on the voice of God, is afraid of the voice of God. An unexpected voice from heaven is disruptive and disorderly. Its very unpredictability is unnerving. A stable and organized community cannot well tolerate individuals who claim to have received a divine communication.

There is an unspoken but real conflict between the spirituality which seeks to hear the voice of God, and the religious authority which seeks to maintain orderliness among its people. The two tendencies may maintain an uneasy truce, or may erupt in conflict. There is a tension between prophets and priests; mystics and rationalists.

The Talmud records a story which is a landmark in Jewish religious history (Baba Metsiah 59 a-b). Rabbi Eliezer and his colleagues (2nd century C.E.) became involved in a debate over the ritual purity of an oven owned by someone named Okhnai. Rabbi Eliezer argued that the oven was ritually clean, while the sages ruled it to be unclean. Since rabbinic law follows the opinion of the majority, Rabbi Eliezer's opinion was overruled. But the rabbi insisted that he was in the right. "If I am correct," he told his colleagues, "let the current of the river outside reverse itself." The current reversed itself. Unimpressed, the rabbis maintained their decision in spite of the miracle. Rabbi Eliezer again challenged: "If I am correct, let the walls of the study hall shake." The walls shook. But the rabbis remained adamant. Finally, Rabbi Eliezer called out: "If I am correct, let a voice from heaven affirm my ruling." A voice from heaven then resounded in approval of Rabbi Eliezer's point of view. But the sages still clung to their decision, retorting that the Torah is "not in heaven." Once God had given the Torah to Israel, He no longer had any authority to intervene in its explication. He had delegated that right to the sages, and it was they who could decide how the law was to be applied. Even when a heavenly voice expressed God's viewpoint on a halakhah, the sages are obliged to follow their own reasoning and not abdicate their responsibility to the divine voice. The law, though based on revelation, is to be maintained by reason.

The Talmudic story relates that shortly after the case of Okhnai's oven, a rabbi met the prophet Elijah and asked him how God had reacted to the rabbis who ignored the heavenly voice. Elijah responded that God was delighted: "My children have been victorious over me," God had stated with pride.

This story, which has had a profound influence on halakhic thought for centuries, indicates that the voice of God is no longer needed or wanted for the resolution of religious questions. On the contrary, religious life is far more organized and predictable when left to human planning.

In line with this attitude is the statement of Maimonides that a prophet has no more authority in Jewish law than any other sage. If a rabbinic court voted on a particular matter and the prophets were all of one opinion while the rabbis were all of the opposite opinion, the law was determined by majority rule. No extra authority is given to the prophets in halakhah.[4]

It is understandable why the sages overruled the power of prophecy. The halakhah could not be left to heavenly voices without undermining rabbinic authority. The law had to be established based on the majority view of intelligent, rational and learned rabbis. If a prophet or heavenly voice were allowed to override the rabbinical decisions, the law would become too tentative. There was always the possibility of someone speaking in the name of God that the law was different. It is not divine truth in the absolute sense which is needed for law; it is concensus among the authoritative legislators of the law.

The voice of God did not stop with the decision of Rabbi Eliezer's colleagues. Certainly, the attitude which they manifested did come to prevail in the halakhah. The Talmudic statement that "a sage is greater than a prophet" became an axiom of religious life.

But outside the domain of halakhah, individuals were still moved by the voice of God. Jewish tradition includes the experiences of spiritually elevated people who received divine messages, whose lives were lived in a personal direct relationship with God.

Messages from Heaven

The city of Safed in northern Israel was a haven for mystics and pietists during the 16th century.[5] Many of these religiously inspired people were victims or children of victims of the expulsion of Jews from Spain in 1492. They came to Israel because it was the Holy Land, the land of prophecy, the land where the Messiah would come to redeem all of the Jewish people.

In the milieu of Safed, individuals longed to hear the voice of God. They attempted to attune their minds and spirits to the heavenly messages which they believed were constantly being transmitted. One of the foremost sages of the Safed community was Rabbi Hayyim Vital, and he described five ways in which a person could obtain divine inspiration.[6]

One could be moved by the holy spirit of God Himself, or through the souls of departed saints, or angels known as *maggidim*, or Elijah the prophet, or dreams. Divine messages came to those who were worthy of receiving them and who were receptive to them. Through piety and asceticism, one could come to cling to God and to draw God's spirit into him. Vital indicated a number of preparations which enabled one to receive the holy spirit. These included repentence for all sins, careful observance of all commandments—particularly prayer and love of one's fellow human beings—physical purification through ritual immersions and by wearing clean clothes. Finally, he recommended silence and solitude, especially after midnight. Once a person had accomplished these requirements, he should "close his eyes, withdraw his mind from all worldly things as if his soul had left the body and he was insensible like a dead corpse. Thereafter he should make an effort to meditate with great passion on a higher world and to cleave there to the roots of his soul and to the supernal lights. He should imagine in his mind as if his soul has left him and was ascending on high, and he should picture the higher world as if he actually stood there. And if he performs any *yihud*, he should intend thereby to draw the light and the influx down on all the world and also intend to receive his own share in the end." If in spite of these exercises, he still does not receive the illumination from God, it is a sign that he is not yet worthy. He should continue to prepare himself.

Vital warns that even if an individual attains a prophetic state, his initial illuminations may be uneven and irregular. It will not always be easy to determine whether one is receiving a true revelation or only an illusion of one. Vital observes: "Know that at first the spirit will come upon him as if by accident, on rare occasion only, and also the contents of the revelations will be slight, not profound, and moreover little in quantity. But as he continues his power will increase."

The voice of God could be transmitted through *maggidim*, angelic speakers. There was a belief among mystics that every word uttered by a person leads to the creation of an angel. An individual who devotes himself to piety and speaking the words of Torah, thereby creates many good angels. These angels "are the mystery of the *maggidim*, and everything depends on the measure of one's good works." A *maggid* could manifest itself through automatic speech, its voice coming though the mouth of the person who is to receive the message. Or it could find other ways of making itself heard.

Rabbi Hayyim Yosef David Azulai, in his book *Shem Hagedolim* mentions a number of scholars and rabbis who received messages from *maggidim*. In popular tradition, saintly people were believed to be visited by the prophet Elijah as well as by angels. Divine voices were available to those who had the capacity and saintliness to receive them.

The Case of Rabbi Yosef Karo

The world of supernatural voices and the world of technical halakhic legalism merged in the unusual personality of Rabbi Yosef Karo (1488–1575). Rabbi Karo is best known for his works on Jewish law: the Shulhan Arukh, the Beit Yosef, his commentary on Maimonides' Mishneh Torah, his responsa. It can be well argued that no other author in Jewish history has made more notable contributions to halakhah.

Yet, Rabbi Karo also wrote a much less well-known volume, *Maggid Mesharim*, which is a kind of diary of messages he received from a heavenly *maggid*. This book offers an entirely different aspect of the mind of the author of the Shulhan Arukh. The rational halakhist and the mystical pietist merge in this one man in a remarkable fusion of these two religious tendencies.

While still living in Turkey (early 16th century), Yosef Karo and some of his colleagues met on the eve of Shabuoth to spend the night learning Torah as was the custom. Among the participants in that study session was Rabbi Shelomo Alkabets, a noted mystic and poet. Alkabets described an unusual event which occurred that evening in a letter.[7] While Yosef Karo was studying, his mouth suddenly opened and words emerged; but the voice was not his. Those present watched and listened in amazement as the voice told them that God approved of their piety and their dedication to Torah; it also urged them to leave Turkey to settle in the land of Israel. From this time, the *maggid* became a regular companion of Karo, visiting him often and giving him many instructions.

The *maggid* revealed itself to Karo at different times, but seemed to prefer the hours after midnight or the early morning, especially Shabbat morning. The *maggid* appeared as the embodiment of the Mishnah, but also represented the divine presence of God. As a rule, it appeared when Karo was alone.

The heavenly voice prodded Rabbi Karo to intense piety.

In one of its early messages, it presented a series of instructions: think only of the Torah and the commandments at all times. Clear your mind of everything else. Pray with intense concentration. Do not engage in empty conversation. Do not laugh. Even if you hear a joke, hold back your laughter and remain serious. Do not become angry over mundane matters. Do not eat too much. Refrain from overeating on the Sabbath. Be exceedingly humble. Always be engaged in repentence. Do not think of women.

The *maggid* promised great things for Yosef Karo. The rabbi was assured that if he constantly thought of the Mishnah and Torah, then "behold, I will make you a prince over my people." The *maggid* promised Karo fame, universal authority in halakhah, success in his yeshiva (rabbinic academy). The *maggid* advised Karo to cling always to God, "and you will merit having miracles be performed by you just as they were performed by those who came earlier."

When Karo had overslept one Sabbath morning, not having woken up until dawn, the *maggid* chastised him for being lazy. It stated that Karo would have to improve himself and mend his ways if he wanted further revelations. Yet, even as the *maggid* criticized Karo, it also encouraged him, telling him that he would learn the secrets of the Torah from Elijah the prophet, face to face.

In a strange promise, the *maggid* assured Karo that he would "be privileged to rise as a burnt offering before me and to be burned for the sanctification of my Name." The idea of martyrdom by burning at the stake for the glory of God was part of the spiritual life of the time, especially in light of the cruelties of the Spanish Inquisition. To a sensitive, kabbalistically inclined person, it was thought to be a tremendous honor to give one's total being to God. Giving up one's physical life for the spiritual life of the afterworld is not a difficult jump in reason.

Interestingly, the *maggid* was primarily concerned with moral guidance and with theoretical kabbalistic concepts. It seldom taught Karo halakhah. Nowhere does Karo assert authority for his legal works on the basis of the fact that he had received divine guidance. Professor Zvi Werblowsky, in his insightful biography of Karo, concluded that "his charismatic or mystical life did not spill over into his daylight activities. The Karo of the codes and the responsa remained healthy, realistic, and down to earth."[8]

But it is not necessary to make a clear dichotomy between the two aspects of Karo's personality. In fact, it may be impossible to understand the significance of his legal works without reference to his mystical spiritual life.

Karo longed to hear divine voices and was blessed with a *maggid* who fulfilled this function. Yet, everyone cannot merit receiving such personal revelations. For religious Jews, the voice of God is reflected in the Torah and the sacred writings. Halakhah, the way God wants us to live, brings us into a living relationship with the voice of God—even if we cannot hear it directly.

Therefore, Karo's legal works are actually attempts to capture and record the voice of God which has been revealed to the people of Israel from the time of Moses. Whereas the *maggid* is a direct and present voice, the halakhah is a "recording" of a voice which can be replayed again and again. Through the study and observance of the Torah and halakhah, a Jew can put his life into the context of God's voice. As one advances in Torah study and observance, he might merit receiving a personal revelation. Legalism and mysticism need not be two disparate entities. They are really inter-related and inter-dependent. At the root, both are listening anxiously for the voice of God.

The Voice of God Today

For many years it has been unfashionable in the West to listen for the voice of God, to engage in mystical thought and meditation. The virtues stressed were rationalism, skepticism, positivism. Individuals who have been dissatisfied with these "virtues" have sought outlets in Eastern religions and in various religious cults.

Purifying religion of the mystical, the spontaneous voice of God, the element of saintliness—this is not purification at all. Rather, it strips religion of its real soul and meaning. Any religious movement that cannot produce truly saintly people who truly believe themselves constantly to be in the presence of God is a false and corrosive movement. Attempts to "modernize" or "rationalize" religion ultimately undermine real religious sentiment.

Essentially, religion must help one be attuned to the voice of God. This is religion's goal. In Jewish teaching, the voice of God is received through special revelations, through the Torah and through halakhah. According to rabbinic tradition, the voice of God calls out to us each day. The gift of Jewish spirituality is to listen for this voice.

8. | TRANSCENDING THE SELF

Think of experiences in your life where you lost your sense of ego, where you transcended yourself and felt part of something greater. Such experiences, which occur to everyone, strike us suddenly, spontaneously. We cannot calculate and prepare ourselves for them. They simply happen to us.

An illustration of this kind of experience is falling in love. Popular language reflects the power of love to overcome us, and we speak of "falling" in love rather than of directing ourselves into it. The notion of being lovesick goes back at least to the Song of Songs. Someone in love feels a tremendous longing for the beloved, and feels incomplete by himself.

In his *Dialogues of Love*, Judah Abrabanel writes that: "The proper definition of the perfect love of a man for a woman is: the conversion of the lover into the beloved together with a desire for the conversion of the beloved into the lover. And when such love is equal on both sides, it is defined as a conversion of each lover into the other."[1] Abrabanel writes that love is supra-rational. It cannot be restrained by reason. In a romantic lament, he describes the state of being in love: "What else can I tell you, save that the lover's part is a continual death in life and life in death? But what I find even more astounding is that, unbearable and overwhelming as is such a lot in its cruelty and tribulations, yet his mind neither hopes nor desires nor designs to escape it, but even holds for his mortal foe whoever counsels or succors him."[2]

There are, of course, other experiences which make us feel that we have gone beyond ourselves, out of ourselves. Sometimes we are particularly moved by music (or other art forms). The music takes hold of us; our hearts jump, our minds drift into it. For those few moments, we experience an ineffable ecstasy. But this experience comes upon us; we cannot plan for it in advance. If we listen to Beethoven's Fifth Symphony in the expectation that we will be powerfully moved, then we cannot be powerfully moved by it. We can only be disappointed; or pretend to be moved. A concert hall might be filled with thousands of people; yet the experience of transcendance, of drifting into the music, may occur only to a few of them, for different reasons, and in different ways.

There are other occasions when we might feel that we have transcended ourselves. Observing the awesome beauty and grandeur of snow-covered mountains; or a star-filled sky at midnight; or the steady churning of ocean waves—these, and other experiences of nature's grandeur, can draw us out of ourselves. For a special moment we lose ourselves in the experience, become one with what we are seeing and feeling. For an instant, we abandon the concepts of subject and object, but rather feel part of the totality of the experience. There is real and profound unity between ourselves and the world. Such feelings may also occur during prayer or sacred meditation.

Moreover, we might lose our sense of self when caught in the frenzy of a crowd. Our identity merges into the organism of the crowd, so that we are swept along within a greater reality than our own private ego. And, certainly there are other occasions in life when people experience transcending their egos.

The fulfillment of spiritual life is the feeling of union with God. The moment of religious understanding gives one the sense that he has gone beyond himself. But this religious experience, like falling in love and the other experiences mentioned before, happens of itself. There is no path that, if followed, will automatically lead to this experience of God. The role of religious observance and meditation, therefore, is to provide us with spiritual receptivity, so that we will be ready for the experience when it does come. One cannot force such a religious experience to happen, any more than one can force himself to fall in love.

Love of God

The Torah teaches a seemingly paradoxical lesson (Deuteronomy, 6:5): "And you will love the Lord your God with all your heart, with all your soul and with all your might." This verse is generally taken to be a positive commandment to love God. Yet, such a commandment is problematic. Love cannot be commanded. All we can do is prepare ourselves to love, and hope that we will indeed love. But if we are required to love, we will face insurmountable obstacles.

The verse in Deuteronomy might be understood not so much as a commandment to love God, but as a statement of the consequences of living a spiritually sensitive life. If one observes God's commandments, studies the Torah, teaches the Torah to his children etc., then it will happen that "you will love the Lord your God with all your heart, with all your soul and with all your might." The result of one's religious preparation and sensitivity will be the blessing of actual love of God with the totality of his being—heart, soul, might.

Jewish mystical tradition has described a framework for spirituality which results in creating receptivity to "fall in love" with God. Jewish mystics developed a variety of techniques to enable themselves to become open to spiritual experience.[3] Among the techniques have been the repetition of particular verses or words, parallel to the use of mantras in Eastern meditation. Kabbalists also involved themselves in writing certain Hebrew words and then permuting the letters in various combinations. Through these and other methods of intense concentration, one stops thinking about the specific words he is saying or writing, and his mind becomes free, open and receptive. He clears his mind, so to speak, to make room for the religious experience.

Aside from such techniques, Kabbalists found value in solitude. Rabbi Eliezer Azikri (16th century Safed) has written that " . . . one day a week, a person should distance himself from others and be alone with himself and his Master; he should attach his thoughts to Him as though he is already standing before Him on the day of judgement. He should speak to God, blessed be He, with soft words as a slave speaks to his master and a son to his father."[4] In another passage, Azikri writes that when the pious ones were in solitude, they removed from their minds the matters of this world and attached their thoughts to the Master of all. He recommends that solitude should be practiced once a week, or once in fifteen days, or at least once a month.[5]

Some rabbis in 16th century Safed had the custom of wandering from place to place, almost at random. Rabbi Mosheh Cordovero and Rabbi Shelomo Alkabets used to practice this technique. Their conversations were described in a book known as "Sefer Gerushin."[6] Cordovero mentions that on their wanderings they received great insights into the meaning of verses in Scripture. These insights came of themselves, without any reflection whatsoever. Cordovero stresses the suddenness and spontaneousness of these insights. "The words of the Torah shined within us and were said of themselves."[7] The wandering served as the technique which heightened receptivity; but the actual experience came of itself.

Jewish mystical thinking has understood that religious observances and meditation serve as the ground from which love of God springs. By creating a thoughtful mood, they help one become receptive to a deep relationship of love with God.

The Kabbalists created religious imagery based on human experiences in which people transcend their egos—the imagery of falling in love, for example. The Song of Songs, which on the surface appears to be a beautiful example of love poetry between a man and a woman, has been seen at least since the days of Rabbi Akiba as a love story between God and the people of Israel. The very lucid, physical imagery of The Song of Songs is transmuted into spiritual imagery. The underlying message is that one loves God in an analogous fashion to the way a man loves a woman. Rabbi Mosheh Cordovero, as well as many others, referred to the community of Israel as the "spouse of the Holy One, blessed be He."[8] The imagery used by mystical thinkers is often quite straightforward. Judah Abrabanel has written: "As we know His perfection, though incapable of apprehending it completely, so we love and desire to enjoy Him in the most perfect union of knowledge possible to us. This great love and desire of ours ravishes us into such contemplation, as exalts our intellect, till, illuminated by special favor of God, it transcends limits of human capacity and speculation, and attains to such union and copulation with God Most High, as proves our intellect to be rather a part of the essence of God, than understanding of merely human form."[9]

One of the beautiful Hebrew poems popularly sung even today is "Yedid Nefesh," by Rabbi Eliezer Azikri. This poem describes the author's lovesickness for God. His soul longs to be in the presence of God. He refers to God as the "Beloved of the soul." The second stanza begins: "Majestic, Beautiful, Radiance of the universe—my soul is sick for Your love."

Love imagery was also utilized to describe the relationship of Israel and the Sabbath. In Rabbi Shelomo Alkabets' famous poem, "Lekha Dodi", the Sabbath is described as a bride. In fact, this poem has been incorporated into the Friday evening services of Jews throughout the world. We greet the Sabbath with the words: "Come my beloved, to greet the bride; let us receive the face of the Sabbath." The imagery of love and marriage is highlighted in a number of traditions. For example: it is customary in some communities to recite the Song of Songs prior to the Friday evening service. In this way, the love relationship between God and Israel is placed in the context of the love relationship between Israel and Shabbat. The Talmudic recommendation of marital intercourse on Friday nights has been understood within the mystical tradition as a physical symbol of the spiritual marriage between God and Israel, Shabbat and Israel. Love imagery is particularly noticeable in the prayer books following the custom of Rabbi Isaac Luria.

Music

The power of music to move and elevate people has been well understood within Jewish religious tradition. The chants and melodies of the synagogue liturgy have a life of their own, quite apart from the meaning of the words which they carry. Some of the most intense and spiritually moving music occurs not in the synagogue, but at the Sabbath meals at home. The *Zemirot* (songs) of the Sabbath, sung at the festive Sabbath meals, must be counted among the most powerful emotive forces in Jewish religious life. This music achieves its height among those who are able to give themselves to it, without inhibition or self-consciousness.

Some years ago I had occasion to attend a "tish" in Meah Shearim in Jerusalem. The *tish* is a gathering on Friday evening at the synagogue-study hall, in which the rebbi—the spiritual leader of the community—presides, and shares of his holiness with the members of his community. I remember that Friday night vividly. I came to the synagogue as an outsider, a Westerner, a doctoral student in an American university. My separateness from the community I visited was manifested in an obvious symbol: I wore a white straw hat, since it was a warm summer evening. Everyone else who wore hats wore black hats. It had to be clear to everyone, even to me, that I was an observer from another civilization, not one of the members of this community.

There was a large table in the room. Sometime before the rebbi arrived, a set of bleachers was placed on either side of the table. Young boys of the community ascended these bleachers and stood on the various rungs. The rebbi arrived and went to the head of the table as his followers gathered around in haste. As it happened, I stood at the opposite end of the table from the rebbi so I could see him without impediment; and no one asked me to move. The rebbi donned a prayer shawl and pulled it over his head. The young men on the bleachers started to chant a wordless song. As they sang, the rest of the people in the room began to hum along. The boys closed their eyes and began to sway and rock with their music. The intensity increased, and I felt myself swaying with the rhythm. After a while, the rebbi made a motion and the group stopped singing. His eyes were closed, his facial expression was tight and eager. He put the prayer shawl to his eyes, and I had the impression that he was crying. When he did this, the singing began once again with an incredible intensity. The young men swayed and bowed, their earlocks flying in every direction. As the singing continued, I closed my eyes and tried to let myself join the spirit in the room. Though always an outsider, I let myself participate in the spiritual life of the community and its music, if only for an instant. But that instant has continued to be important and sacred to me.

Anyone who has allowed himself/herself to enter the spirituality of religious music understands this feeling. Whether it be at a *tish* in Meah Shearim, or a Friday evening meal at a yeshiva, or in a spiritually alive synagogue, or at the Shabbat table of religiously great people—the power of music to elevate us is truly remarkable. It is not surprising, then, that music has played a vital role in Jewish spirituality over the ages.

Prayer

Prayer—whether private or public—is an expression of a human being directed towards God. The words of prayer may express thanksgiving, praise of God, pleas for help.

Prayers may be uttered spontaneously, or may be repetitions of ancient prayer texts, hallowed by centuries of repetition.

Yet, doesn't it seem arrogant for finite human beings to address an infinite and eternal God? What claim can any of us have on God's concern? What right do we have to assume that our lives are so significant that we may ask God to heal us when we are sick, give us strength when we are weak, provide us with all our needs and wants? And how can we find adequate words to express ourselves to God? Inevitably, our words must fall far short of their goal.

And yet, we pray. In spite of the above questions, we feel perfectly natural in bringing our petitions, praises and words of thanksgiving to God. The Bible itself is our precedent. Our ancestors prayed and they were answered. We pray, therefore, not from a rational philosophical justification but from a deeply felt natural human need.

Prayer is inspired by two different emotions: love and fear. Moses Maimonides has written (*Mishneh Torah: Madda* 2:2): "When a person contemplates His great and wondrous acts and creations, obtaining from them a glimpse of His wisdom which is beyond compare and is infinite, he will promptly love and glorify Him, longing exceedingly to know the great Name of God. As David said: 'My whole being thirsts for God, the living God' (Psalms, 42:3). And when he ponders these very subjects, he will be afraid and will recoil, knowing that he is a lowly and obscure creature . . . as David said: 'As I look up to the Heavens Your fingers made . . . what is man that You should be mindful of him?' (Psalms 8:4–5)."

The spiritual context of religion—and therefore of prayer—is dynamic. It fluctuates between feelings of love and feelings of fear, awareness of the spiritual greatness of human beings and awareness of our profound insignificance.

This spiritual tension is an essential feature of Jewish prayer. The morning and evening services both include the recitation of the *Shema*, the classic Biblical text affirming the unity/uniqueness of God. The *Shema* is preceded by two prayers, each of which culminates with a blessing of God. Although the actual texts differ from morning to evening services, and also differ from Sabbath and holidays to weekdays, their themes are identical. The first blessing praises God as Creator, the Almighty Being who oversees the entire universe, whose power is overwhelming. This blessing evokes fear and reverence in us. We are humbled by our own smallness in relationship to Almighty God. The second blessing, however, focuses on God's love of Israel. It evokes within us a feeling of closeness to God. Its mood contrasts sharply with that of the previous blessings.

After having experienced both moods—fear and love— then the Shema is recited, illustrating that God is One. Our contrasting experiences of God, first as the Almighty Creator and then as a loving compassionate God, merge into our greater perception of God's unity. The structure of the prayers leads one to recognize the surprising tension inherent in prayer as well as the surprising satisfaction from unifying dissonant perceptions.

There has always been a tendency for people to develop prayer formulae, in the hope that by repeating these magic words God will do what the worshipper wants him to do. Prayer of this type is akin to magic. It is particularly appealing to people who tend to be superstitious, or who feel the urge to control God.

Rabbinic tradition has referred to prayer as "the service of the heart." It transcends the recitation of incantations. Its goal is not to control God, but to give oneself to God. Prayer is the expression of a sensitive and thoughtful soul.

The great Kabbalist, Rabbi Isaac Luria, taught that it was forbidden for a person to say his prayers in sadness.[10] Rather, a person who prays should feel joy, exaltation. Without this joy, the soul lacks the power to receive enlightenment from above by means of his prayer. Even when one offers prayers with deep humility, he must always retain a great joy at the same time.

In listing the laws of prayer, Rabbi Yosef Karo includes the following rules in his *Shulhan Arukh* (O.H. Chapter 93): "A person should wait one hour before rising to pray, in order to direct his heart towards God. A person should not rise to pray except with fear and humility; not from the midst of laughter, nor lightheadedness, nor vain matters, nor from the midst of anger. Rather (he should pray) from the midst of joy . . ."

An essential feature of prayer is *kavvanah*, concentration. In the laws of prayer (O.H. chapter 98), the *Shulhan Arukh* states: "One who prays must concentrate his heart on the meaning of the words which are uttered from his lips. He should imagine that the Shekhinah is opposite him. He should remove all thoughts that trouble him until his thought and concentration are pure in his prayer . . . and thus did the pious and saintly people: they meditated and concentrated on their prayers until they reached the level of transcending physicality and elevating the power of the mind until they reached near the level of prophecy . . . "

Prayer on its highest level, then, is a devotion of love which unites the worshipper with God. Judah Abrabanel, in describing the nature of love, provides a description which very well complements the words of Rabbi Karo concerning prayer. Abrabanel writes: "But when the mind retires within itself to contemplate most earnestly and most closely unite with a beloved subject, it recedes from the external parts of the body, and abandons both sense and movement, gathering to itself for this meditation, the greater part of its faculties and spirits. Only that power is left without which the life of the body could not be maintained: to wit, the vital power, by virtue of which the heart is kept in perpetual motion and the spirits breathe through the arteries . . . "[11]

Prayer on this spiritual level is not easy to attain on a regular basis. It should be noted, furthermore, that the spiritual effect of the recitation of prayers is not necessarily tied to the contents of the prayers themselves. For example, the recitation of an ancient Hebrew prayer—hallowed by centuries of tradition—may move the worshipper by the mystery of the words, the melody, the historical association. Translating such a prayer into the vernacular might make its contents more understandable, but at the same time take away the spiritual power of that prayer. For example, the Kaddish, chanted in Aramaic by mourners, has a life all its own quite separate from the meaning of its words. Since the kaddish has been recited for centuries by mourners, its deep association with mourning and respect for the dead has a powerful emotive influence on the one who recites it. This is not to advocate that prayers should not be understood for their content. Rather, it is only to say that the meaning and power of a prayer vastly transcend the literal translation of its words.

It is customary in many Jewish communities, particularly among Sephardim, for pious people to read passages from the Zohar as part of their religious lives. The Zohar is considered to be a sacred volume, containing the ultimate mysteries and truths of the Kabbalah. Many pious people read the Zohar, even without the faintest understanding of the meaning of the words they chant. Yet, this very reading imbues them with an overwhelming spirituality and sense of closeness to God. Rabbi Hayyim Yosef David Azulai expressed a wide-spread belief when he wrote: "The study of the Zohar is above any other study, even if one doesn't understand what it says, and even if he errs in his reading. It is a great corrective for the soul. Even though the Torah is composed of the names of God, nevertheless it is clothed in a number of stories. One who reads and understands the stories pays attention to the obvious meaning. But the book of the Zohar is composed of the ultimate mysteries themselves, revealed. One who reads them knows that they are the mysteries and secrets of the Torah though they are not understood due to the shortcomings of the perceiver and the profundity of that which is being perceived."[12]

Humility

Through meditation and prayer, a person can transcend his ego. In fact, one's awareness of himself is an obstacle to spirituality. When an artist, for example, becomes self-conscious while creating a work of art—that very self-consciousness creates artificiality and falseness. It is precisely when an artist is so immersed in his work that he loses his self-awareness that his work is spontaneous and authentic. The ego does not become a barrier between the artist and his art. Likewise in prayer and meditation: it is authentic when it is deep and unifying, when the ego does not intercede between the person and God.

Humility, therefore, is at the root of true spirituality. A humble person is willing to surrender his ego to the religious experience. It may be argued that the many references in the prayer book to our sinfulness are not there to make us feel guilty; but rather, to make us aware of our need for humility. The confessions of our sins are not meant to make us feel that we are bad and unworthy; but rather that we ought not be arrogant and egocentric. We should have no qualms at admitting our shortcomings.

Bahya Ibn Pakuda wrote in his "Duties of the Heart," that "the primary condition for the service of God is that the worshipper should free himself from the spirit of domination." He wrote that a human being's service of God "can only exist when he assumes all the conditions of servitude— humility and lowliness before God, and rids himself of all forms of domination—grandeur, dignity, haughtiness, self-glory, pride, majesty and any similar feeling. . . . this service can only be rendered correctly if humility and lowliness before God and submissiveness to Him are genuine. . . . hence it follows that all moral qualities are secondary to humility which is the head and front of them all. It also logically follows that no moral quality can possibly exist in anyone whose heart is devoid of humility before God or has in it aught of pride, haughtiness or conceit."[13]

Mosheh Hayyim Luzzatto, in discussing the means of acquiring humility, quotes rabbinic attitudes on humility. "A sign of pride is poverty of Torah" (Sanhedrin 24a). "A sign of complete ignorance is self-praise" (Zohar Balak).[14]

Obviously, if one thinks he is humble—he probably is not humble. Humility can be pretentious, in which case it is not true humility at all. Humility does not mean acting in a subservient and docile fashion; it does mean that a human being is aware of his limitations, of the fact that he is created from dust and will return to dust. This calm wisdom keeps one from taking himself too seriously. It allows him the freedom to transcend insults and petty words of disrespect from others.

Rabbi Mosheh Cordovero has taught that a person should learn humility from God Himself.[15] God constantly nourishes everything: even a human being who is sinning against God is sustained by God. God bears the insult and still does good to the one who insults him. Men should follow this virtue. Be patient. Even if insulted, one should not refuse to bestow his goodness. "The quality of humility includes all qualities, for it belongs to the Crown which is the highest attribute." The Crown always looks down, because it is ashamed to look up at its Source. "So too man should be ashamed to gaze proudly upwards, but he should ever look downwards in order to abase himself as much as possible."

Cordovero states that a person can accustom himself to being humble, little by little. First, a person should flee honor as much as possible. Second, a person should be aware of his own unworthiness. Third, one should be aware of his sins.

Another way to learn humility is to honor all creatures, recognizing in them the exalted nature of the Creator. Love your fellow-man, even the wicked. Humility means being truly open to the experience of life.

Jewish tradition has drawn on the powerful emotive forces which lead one to transcend his ego: love, music, nature, prayer and meditation. It has stressed humility as the primary virtue. It was Moses, after all, who was described as the most humble man in the Torah; and it was also Moses who alone saw God "face to face."

9. | PROVIDENCE

The Torah describes God as the Creator of the universe, and also as the Being Who oversees and is involved in the lives of the Biblical characters. God is an active participant in human affairs. He responds to prayers; he reveals Himself to individuals and to the entire people of Israel; he offers rewards and punishments. God is definitely not understood in the Torah as an abstract force or principle.

Jewish spirituality presupposes a providential God. Human beings are not meaningless automatons, but are the creations of God. Each person has the possibility of elevating himself spiritually so as to enter a personal relationship with God. Moses Maimonides has posited that the higher one's level of intellectual understanding of God, the more providence God showers on him.[1] But whether or not we accept Maimonides' position, the fact remains that people experience the providence of God in different ways.

One of the persistent problems in religious philosophy deals with the nature of God's providence. Since we like to believe that God is fair and just, why does God sometimes act in ways that seem to be unfair and unjust? Why do innocent people suffer? Why do wicked people prosper? Why does Providence not so manage the affairs of humanity so that the righteous are always rewarded and the wicked always punished?

Elements within Jewish tradition underscore the human assumption that God must act justly. For example, when God decided to destroy the wicked citizens of Sodom, He first informed Abraham of His intention. But Abraham offered an objection. Perhaps some righteous people lived in Sodom. Surely God would not destroy the righteous along with the wicked! "Will the Judge of all the world not do justice?" God surrendered to Abraham's argument, and finally agreed not to destroy the city if even ten righteous people could be found there. The Torah reports that the city was destroyed, but only after Lot and his family (the righteous of the city) were given the chance to escape.

The notion that God must act justly is evident in much rabbinic literature. "The Almighty does not deal despotically with His creatures" (Abodah Zarah 3a) is a formulation of this assumption.

Yet, this pattern does not always seem to be followed in human history. Innocent lives are lost daily; good people are not given opportunities to escape every evil. Our assumption that God is just and merciful often collides with the reality we experience, the evidence of our own eyes.

The Talmud (Gittin 56b) records a dramatic confrontation between our assumption and reality. The Second Temple was destroyed by the Roman general, Titus. The Talmud relates the horrible deeds of Titus. Jews were slaughtered, sold into slavery, exiled. Titus is characterized as a vicious tyrant, lacking in mercy and respect. The Jews who experienced the destruction of the Temple and the downfall of the Jewish state were in a state of spiritual disarray. It seemed inconceivable that God would allow a cruel, godless Roman to massacre and defeat the Jews, the chosen people of God. Innocent men, women and children were killed or abused. The suffering was overwhelming.

The Jewish religious response to the catastrophe was imbued with perplexity and anger. Scriptural verses which sang the praise of God were re-interpreted by several rabbis to read as criticisms of God. For example, Psalm 89 extols God and asks: "Who is like You in strength, oh God?" Abba Hanan interpreted the verse to mean: "Who is like You, so strong and hard, that You hear the curses and blasphemies of that wicked person [Titus] and yet You are silent?" The school of Rabbi Ishmael offered an even more startling piece of exegesis. Exodus 15 includes the verse: "Who is like You among the mighty [elim], oh God?" The interpretation is: "Who is like You among mutes (ilemim) oh God?" God witnessed all the evil which occurred and yet remained silent as innocent blood was spilled. How could He have withheld intervention?

This reaction is paralleled in several elegies composed after the expulsion of Jews from Spain in 1492.[2] One of them begins:

> Alas, our Father, is this the recompense
> we have sought?
> Who is the father who raises children
> to take vengeance on them,
> to pour anger on them
> with great and fuming wrath?
> We have sat on the ground, we have also wept.

The poem continues as a dialogue between Israel and God. Israel objects that God had allowed them to suffer so much and so unfairly. God responds that the sufferings are a result of Israel's own sins. Israel retorts—even if we have sinned, God is supposed to be merciful and forgiving. Moreover, even if some have sinned, can God believe that the children are all guilty to deserve such suffering? The dialogue continues until God finally concedes that He will restore Israel, will rebuild the Temple in Jerusalem, and fully redeem the Jews. The author of this elegy, which was incorporated in the service for the Ninth of Av in many Sephardic communities, insists that God admit His unjustness in His dealings with Israel. God must make recompense for His unfairness.

The above examples reflect anger and incredulity at God's apparent lack of justness. They assume that God must be righteous and must be held responsible for any injustices which occur in the world. They are manifestations of a spiritual double bind, a situation where two opposite truths conflict with each other, leaving us confused and frustrated. One truth is that God is providential, compassionate and just; the other truth is that many good people suffer, innocent people die prematurely. There are no evident distinctions between the wicked and the righteous; blessings and curses are distributed among people haphazardly, not because they were earned. Diseases, natural disasters, genetic defects—these strike at humans without reference to their righteousness or lack thereof. How do we reconcile our assumptions about God with the realities we see daily in human affairs?

Afterlife

In the *Ethics of the Fathers*, Rabbi Yaacov teaches: "This world is like a vestibule to the future world; prepare yourself in the vestibule so you can enter the banquet hall." By righteous living in this temporal life, one earns eternal life in the world to ccme. The vicissitudes of this life should not be taken out of proportion. No matter how great our suffering may be here, we can look forward to eternal bliss after our earthly death. Rabbi Tarfon has taught (also in the *Ethics of the Fathers*): "Know that the righteous receive their reward in the world to come."

These and other similar statements in rabbinic literature try to resolve our human dilemma by stressing the following beliefs: 1) life on earth is temporal, and far less significant than the eternal life in the world to come; 2) if a righteous person suffers here or if a wicked person prospers, this is only a temporary phenomenon. In the world to come, God will reward the righteous and punish the wicked. One should not judge God's ultimate justice by what one sees in this temporal life; one can trust that God's justice will prevail in the next world, which is far more significant than this world.

Rav, a leading rabbi of the third century C.E., described the world to come as a place free of physical wants and needs. "All that the righteous do is to sit with their crowns on their heads and enjoy the radiance of the Divine Presence" (Berakhot 17a). Maimonides believed that the world to come reserved for the righteous entails pure goodness and eternal life. The reward of the righteous will be to enjoy the splendor of God's presence. The closer one comes to God in this world, the more he perfects his understanding—the greater will be his spiritual reward in the next world. One who does not live righteously and does not develop his intellectual and spiritual abilities—such a person will be deprived of sharing the glory of God in the world to come.[3]

In stressing the importance of the world to come, these sources play down the problems which may arise in this world. Our task is to live properly and to experience our relationship with God as best we can. If we suffer adversity, we should not be deterred from our belief in God's goodness and justice; the rewards and punishments are not generally meted out in this world, but in the next.

Messianism

Yet, the Jewish tradition also expresses the belief that God will reward the righteous and punish the wicked even in this world. In messianic times, the righteous will be resurrected from the dead and will enjoy peace and blessing; the wicked will be punished for their sins. In a broader sense, the messianic idea teaches that Israel will ultimately be vindicated. The many sufferings which the Jews have absorbed will be counterbalanced in messianic times by blessings and national freedom.

The messianic belief is based on the assumption that history has a direction, that a providential God gives meaning to human events. Professor Gershom Scholem has indicated different tendencies within Jewish messianic thought: a rational view which sees the messianic era as a natural outgrowth of history; an apocalyptic view which sees it as an abrupt, miraculous break with history.[4] The common denominator of these tendencies is that the messianic idea provided the Jewish people with a hope for better times. It was a dream of an ideal world which would some day come into being as God's way of demonstrating His justness and fairness to Israel.

The role of the messianic idea in Jewish thought needs to be understood not merely as wishful thinking or nationalistic yearning of the people of Israel. It is not simply a faith for victims, a beautiful dream to pacify a suffering people. Rather, it is a belief in the ultimate justness of God.

Jewish eschatology corrects the distortions of reality as humans experience it. God is certainly just; if things do not appear to verify this truth, then we can be assured that somehow history will vindicate God's justness. If history is filled with injustices, redemption will come to rectify history. Righteousness will be rewarded; evil will be punished.

The messianic idea, then, is not simply the hope of the Jewish people, but the demand of the Jewish people. God *must* redeem Israel because Israel has suffered enormously and unfairly. If our eyes do not see God's justness now, we can be sure that the day will come when God's justness is manifest to everyone.

Suffering as a Positive Feature of Life

Suffering in this world can be seen as a positive feature of life. Rabbi Benzion Uziel has written that when we are comfortable and well off, we tend to ignore God's providential rule of our lives. But when we are suffering, our thoughts are awakened and we are brought closer to God. "Suffering (yisu-

rin) awakens us to examine our deeds, to recognize the righteousness of the justice and the correctness of the judgment,
and they give us the expression of our lips for prayer and
supplication, for thanksgiving and praise to the Creator of
man Who created us in justice and Who remembers us in
justice and Who performs kindness for us with justice, with
true justice and righteous justice."[5] Rabbi Uziel argues that it
is precisely those who seem to lack the physical blessings of
this life who are best able to express deep spiritual feelings. A
poor person can pray to God with a pure and full heart, can
reach depths of feeling in his cries to God. Likewise, at times
of grief or illness a person's spiritual sensitivity is expanded.
The sufferings, thus, lead to a higher spiritual level, a level
which would not be reached without adversity.

The Talmudic sage Rabba (some say Rav Hisda) taught: If
a person sees that painful sufferings visit him, let him examine his conduct. If he can find absolutely no reason for him
to be punished, then he can be sure that these are chastenings
of love (Berakhot 5a). Although one may prefer to be spared
these sufferings, they still may elevate his spiritual life.

One of the rabbis of the Talmud was known as Nahum
Gamzo. The name Gamzo was derived from a Hebrew phrase
which he always uttered: Gam zo letovah, this also is for the
best. His philosophy was that everything that God did was for
the best. Since God is perfect, the world and all that is in it are
also perfect. Even things which appear to us as defects are
really good. It is our inadequate understanding that leads us
to think of things as being bad or evil. Our challenge, according to this way of thinking, is to reconcile ourselves to whatever happens, having faith that all that occurs is ultimately
good because it derives from a beneficent providence. Suffering should not be experienced as an evil which God has
inflicted on a person arbitrarily, but as an opportunity for
spiritual growth.

The Mystery of God's Ways

Another way of dealing with the problem of evil in the world is to argue that God's ways are mysterious, beyond our comprehension. Being eternal, God is not bound in any way by our judgments or our reason. When Moses asked God for His name, God told him "Ehyeh asher ehyeh," I am what I am. In other words, God transcends human understanding.

The book of Job presents an interesting treatment of the problem. Job, who is righteous, has his faith tested. His children die, his property is destroyed, and he is afflicted with illness. Three friends visit him and ask him to confess his sins. They believe that it is impossible for anyone to suffer without deserving the punishment. They believe, like Abraham in the story of Sodom, that God is a true judge who acts fairly. Yet, Job denies any guilt. He claims that he is suffering although he has not sinned. But his friends continue to preach to him, tormenting him.

At last, God intercedes. He answers Job out of the tempest (chapter 38): "Where were you when I laid the earth's foundations? Tell me, if you know and understand. Who settled its dimensions? Surely you should know. Who stretched his measuring line over it? On what do its supporting pillars rest? Who set its cornerstone in place, when the morning stars sang together and all the sons of God shouted aloud? Who watched over the birth of the sea, when it burst in flood from the womb? When I wrapped it in a blanket of cloud and cradled it in fog, when I established its bounds, fixing its doors and bars in place . . . "

God describes His enormous power, contrasting it with the powerlessness of human beings. Who controls the weather? Who oversees the lives of the animals? God tells Job: "Brace yourself and stand up like a man. I will ask questions and you shall answer. Dare you deny that I am just or put me in the wrong that you may be right? Have you an arm like God's arm, can you thunder with a voice like His? . . .

Look upon the proud man and humble him; look upon every proud man and bring him low, throw down the wicked where they stand; hide them in the dusk together, and shroud them in an unknown grave. Then I in my turn will acknowledge that your own right hand can save you."

God's speech is a forceful rebuke to humans. He is beyond our judgments. Humans are powerless and lacking in understanding; compared to the all-powerful and all-knowing God, humans are as nothing. We are in no position to criticize or argue with God. We cannot even understand His ways.

The friends of Job were wrong: God does not punish only as a result of one's sins. Good and evil appear in the world as God chooses, not necessarily as results of human behavior. There is no way we can stand in judgment of God.

The Talmud records a story which elaborates on this theme (Menahot 29b). Moses is said to have visited God in heaven and found Him writing a scroll of the Torah. On certain letters, God drew little crowns (taggin), and Moses inquired as to their significance. God informed Moses that there would one day be a rabbi so wise that he would understand the entire Torah, each letter and even each crown. Moses was awed and asked for the opportunity to meet this sage. God transported Moses into the future where he found himself in the back of a crowded classroom in which Rabbi Akiba was delivering a discourse in Jewish law. Moses was overwhelmed by the discussion and had difficulty in understanding the profound teachings of Rabbi Akiba. When Moses returned to God, he asked: Considering the greatness of Akiba, why did You choose to give the Torah to Israel through me? Akiba is a far better choice. God answered: Be silent. This is My decree.

Moses then asked to see the reward which God had in store for Rabbi Akiba. God again transported Moses into the future, where he witnessed Romans weighing Akiba's flesh in the marketplace after he had been cruelly tortured to death.

Moses was stunned. Returning to God, he asked: is this the reward such a righteous man deserves? God answered: be silent; this is My decree.

God acts as He acts. He is not subject to our judgment, our approval or disapproval. If we do not understand His ways, this is our problem, not His. The Talmudic sage, Rabbi Yannai, admitted: "we can not explain either the prosperous security of the wicked nor the sufferings of the virtuous." (Ethics of the Fathers, 4:19).

Attributing Evil to God

There is an understandable aversion to attributing evil to God. Philosophers such as Maimonides have argued that God does not create evil directly, but that evil is simply an absence of good. This is an interesting and subtle philosophic distinction, which is well formulated in "Da'at Tevunot," by M. H. Luzzatto. The argument essentially says that God does not create evil directly. Rather, God created the world through revelation of His spirit and through concealment of His spirit. Not everything shares the same degree of God's spirit. Some are more infused with His spirit, some are less so. Since God, for reasons beyond our understanding, uses direct creation and providence as well as concealment, the continuum of reality has things which are good (more infused with God's direct providence) and things which are less good (towards which God has concealed His presence to some degree). Evil, then, is not an active creation of God; but is a result of God's concealment.[6]

Harold Kushner, unwilling to attribute evil to God, argues that evil happens by itself, and that God has no control to stop it. Kushner believes that it is impossible to believe in a God Who created evil and Who acts unjustly. Therefore, anything that appears as an evil—diseases, natural disasters, etc.—is not within God's domain, but is in the domain of nature over which God has no control.[7]

Yet, the prophet Isaiah had no difficulty in attributing

evil to God. He stated candidly (Isaiah 45:7) that God "forms light and creates darkness; He makes peace and creates evil." This verse in Isaiah, in its full candor, contains the seeds of unravelling the problem which we have been discussing. By comprehending the universe as a unity, containing light and darkness, good and evil—all created by God—Isaiah may be removing the problem altogether.

We have been trying to resolve a double bind. We have two contradictory premises: that God is good, fair, just; and that there is evil in the world. We have considered different ways of alleviating the tension of this dilemma. One set of answers assumes that God is just; the evil is only temporary, or apparent, or it will be balanced by justice in the afterlife and in messianic times. Another set of answers admits that there is evil in the world; that God can do whatever He likes whether or not His actions win our approval; or that God really has no power to stop evil. But none of these answers eliminates the double bind entirely. We are still left with a nagging feeling that the problem is unresolved.

Isaiah's Insight

Isaiah does not attempt to answer our question; rather he tries to eliminate the double bind which creates our spiritual tension. Perhaps our very question is based on wrong assumptions.

God is One. Everything that is—is a manifestation of God. Light and darkness, life and death, growth and decay— all are part of a unity. They are not in opposition to each other, but are in balance with each other.

The Bible states that God saw the world he created and declared it to be very good. Commenting on Genesis 1:31, Rabbi Moses ben Nahman relates an ancient Jewish notion that God was pleased that "the order was very properly arranged since the evil is needed for the preservation of the good, just as it is said, 'To everything there is a season, and a time to every purpose under the heaven.' " In other words, "evil" is a necessary feature of the universe; it is a balance for the "good."

The first chapter of this book pointed out how deeply attached Jewish spirituality is to the natural world. God reveals Himself through the world He created. The universe inspires within us a recognition of God's power, wisdom. When we observe the natural world carefully, we are awed by its intricacy, its orderliness, its vastness, its might.

But if we study the natural world, we also find things which appear cruel. And we find mutations and defects. These aspects of nature are part of the reality of the universe. They are not mistakes. God has formed the world to include these features, and these features are somehow necessary for the balance of nature.

For example, lions eat zebras. To the zebra being torn apart by a hungry lion, the system does not seem fair. Yet, lions must eat zebras as part of the natural order of things. If, out of compassion, we decided to protect zebras from lions, lions would die of starvation and zebras would multiply to an unacceptable level. The natural ecological balance will be upset, plant life will change, food supplies will become altered. An act of seeming compassion would actually be destructive to nature's balance. Lewis Thomas has written quite convincingly that nature has its own "wisdom," its own set of checks and balances.[8] We may have compassion for the zebra being eaten by the lion, but we know without doubt that zebras must be eaten by lions. We may feel grief at the death of an individual person, but we know that everyone must die. We can observe the ways of nature, even though we cannot necessarily explain why the balances are as they are.

The universe contains peace and harmony, but also eruptions and disharmony. Both dimensions are part of the same reality and are part of God's creation. They cannot be understood separately, but only in relationship to each other.

Nature has its own system of operation. Within the system there are things which cause pain and death. Nature does not distinguish between good people and bad people; all are equally subject to bacteria, earthquakes, crippling diseases. Though no one may choose to be a victim of the "evils" of nature, everyone knows that the "evils" are part of nature and that people will inevitably be stricken. Most people will admit this, but will also admit that they would prefer for these things to happen to someone other than themselves and their loved ones.

The question is not one of good and evil. Nature is "neutral." Even the Bible recognizes that nature has its laws and that God does not tamper with them except in extraordinary cases known as miracles. No one can depend on divine intervention to counteract the flow of nature. Normally, nature carries out its set of balances; no one can tamper with these balances without bringing on a whole new set of problems.

Good and evil are not objective realities, but are interpretations which we give to things. When we say that something is good or bad, we are really saying that our opinion of that thing is good or bad. The forces of nature as created by God are neutral; depending on how one is affected by these forces, one will say something is good or something is evil.

For example, suffering is to a large extent determined by the individual who is undergoing the suffering. Outside observers cannot know the truth of the situation but can only project their own feelings. Being in pain may not be considered evil to the person having the pain. Marathon runners often find themselves in tremendous pain, but this does not evoke self-pity or spiritual struggle. On the contrary, the pain is part of a glorious experience. An observer, watching the runner hobbling towards the finish line, may express pity for the poor fellow who is in such agony. But the runner himself may be filled with inexpressible joy in spite of his physical discomfort—a joy that the observer may not even imagine.

A more dramatic example may be drawn from children with Downe's Syndrome. Outsiders may display pity or sym-

pathy for these children, viewing them as unfortunate victims. They may ask why God created "defective" individuals. Yet, within the minds of the children themselves there
may be no self-pity or anger at God. Within their own minds,
they may be the happiest children on earth. They are delighted with the slightest progress they make, they are af-
fectionate and cheerful. Can an outsider fairly judge their true
condition and satisfaction with life and with the God who
created them?

We arrive at the following conclusions: 1) God has
created the universe, with all its features; 2) things which
appear to us to be good or evil are our own perceptions, not
objective descriptions of reality; 3) the natural world which
God created is neutral, making no distinctions based on the
righteousness or wickedness of people; 4) God can defy the
laws of nature, in a miraculous way, but does so very seldom,
and certainly no one has a right to expect miracles on his
behalf.

The Talmud (Hagigah 14b) tells a story of four rabbis
who entered the *pardes*, the sphere of metaphysical speculation. They wanted to understand God's ways, to deal with the
double bind of a good God doing evil. One of the sages died.
One lost his mind. Obviously, the problem was too powerful
for them. Rabbi Elisha ben Abuyah became a heretic; he
concluded that "there is no justice and no Judge." The double
bind could not be resolved, so he gave up his assumption of a
just God. Rabbi Akiba, though, entered the *pardes* in peace
and left in peace. Confronted by the same double bind as the
others, Akiba was yet able to live in peace with his faith. He
realized that the problem itself was based on wrong assumptions, that the universe is a harmonious unity, that the things
we call good and bad are subjective judgments. He recognized the wisdom of Isaiah's statement that God created good
and evil, light and darkness—that the balance of the world
depends on these forces. Evil and good are not mutually
exclusive opposites, but exist in a necessary relationship

with each other. If there were no darkness, light would have no meaning. If there were no death, life would have no meaning. If there were no evil, good would have no meaning. We may not particularly enjoy it when the "evil" elements of the universe are victimizing us or those we love; but we cannot help but realize that these elements are necessary parts of the universe.

Humans do not have a comprehensive view of the universe. We are mortal and finite. God, being beyond time and space, encompasses the mystical unity of the universe. His "perspective" is complete. Lewis Thomas has offered a significant insight, which serves to underscore the difference in comprehending the universe between God and humans. "The individual parts played by other instrumentalists—crickets or earthworms, for instance—may not have the sound of music by themselves, but we hear them out of context. If we could listen to them all at once, fully orchestrated in their immense ensemble, we might become aware of the counterpoint, the balance of tones and timbres and harmonics, the sonorities. The recorded songs of the humpback whale, filled with tensions and resolutions, ambiguities and illusions, incomplete, can be listened to as a *part* of music, like an isolated section of an orchestra. If we had better hearing, and could discern the descants of seabirds, the rhythmical tympani of schools of mollusks, or even the distant harmonics of midges hanging over meadows in the sun, the combined sound might lift us off our feet."[9] What we perceive in fragments, God encompasses in toto. It is an awesome and humbling thought.

Human Evil

Many of the evils which humans complain about are actually created directly by humans, not by God. Violent crimes, wars, air pollution, water contamination, transportation accidents etc.—all are the result of human creativity and freedom. To be sure, God implanted in humans the capacity for doing good and evil, and perhaps even gave evil a bit more sway in the human species. But humans have the freedom to choose to do what is good, kind, compassionate. If they choose to murder, rape, plunder—their evils should not be attributed to God.

The Nazi holocaust has caused considerable spiritual unrest among Jews in recent years. It seems incomprehensible that millions of innocent Jews should have been so methodically and savagely murdered by the Germans and their allies. People ask: where was God? Why did God not intervene? How could God have allowed innocent people to fall victim to cruel and wicked people? How can we hope to understand the tragedy of the destruction of one and a half million children by the Nazis?

And yet, the questions are not properly addressed to God but to humans. God did not create the war. He did not create Nazi ideology, or instill viciousness in them, or build their gas chambers, or load their guns. The horrible thing about the Holocaust was that it was entirely a human creation. It was started by humans, maintained by humans, and was not stopped by humans who should have opposed these horrors.

The Holocaust should inspire us with disgust, anger and even despair—emotions directed against human beings for being capable of such heinous crimes, and for allowing such savagery to take place. We cannot in any fairness blame God for the Holocaust.

But we are bothered by the fact that God remained silent while innocent people were being slaughtered by the millions. We are angry that He did not perform some miracle to change the course of events. But we have no right to expect miracles; life follows its own course and dramatic miracles seldom intervene. That is not God's problem; it is our problem. We need to rely on ourselves, on human resources.

A rabbinic legend teaches that when the Temple in Jerusalem was being razed by the Romans, the Jews were amazed that God could have allowed this to happen. Moreover, they

thought that in recognition of this terrible tragedy the sun
should grow dim. But the sun glowed as usual, giving no
indication at all that the natural world shared in the sadness
of Israel. God taught them that He placed the natural world in
its set order and that it would carry out its laws. No one could
expect these laws to change, in spite of the vicissitudes of
human events.[10]

Although the natural laws prevail and human affairs are
largely left to humans, God's providence does manifest itself
in the lives of individuals, and in the lives of nations.

The Chosenness of Israel

God's providence is evidenced in His covenant with
Israel. God revealed Himself to the Israelites and gave them
the Torah as a guide for their lives. The Torah speaks of Israel
as a chosen people; this chosenness is itself an indication of
God's involvement in the affairs of humans.

That Israel has been selected by God for a unique destiny
is clear; this chosenness becomes more obvious with the
passage of time. The ancient Israelites received the Torah,
were given prophets, and created a religious literature which
has dramatically influenced the course of human history.
The Jews have carried the Torah and its teachings through
the millenia, in many different lands, often under severe
oppression and persecution. Yet, the Torah still impacts on
human life today, and the Jews are still here as living witnesses of God's covenant with ancient Israel. The special
nature of Israel's relationship with God is understood best
through history, not through philosophic speculation.

Rabbi Yehuda Halevy (c. 1075–1141), in his *Kuzari*, has
expressed the idea that God's providence towards Israel is
best evidenced in history.[11] The *Kuzari* is a literary creation
based on a historical foundation. The king of the Khazars felt
the need to follow the true religion. Ultimately, he and many
of his people converted to Judaism. Halevy composed dialogues between the king and sages representing Islam and

Christianity. In both instances, the king was dissatisfied. Finally, he called a Jewish sage and asked about his belief.

The rabbi replied: "I believe in the God of Abraham, Isaac and Israel, who led the children of Israel out of Egypt with signs and miracles; who fed them in the desert and gave them the land, after having made them traverse the sea and the Jordan in a miraculous way; who sent Moses with His law, and subsequently thousands of prophets, who confirmed His law by promises to the observant, and threats to the disobedient. Our belief is comprised in the Torah—a very large domain."

The king objected to this answer. "Now, o Jew, shouldn't you have said that you believed in the Creator of the world, its governor and guide, and in Him who created and keeps you, and such attributes which serve as evidence for every believer, and for the sake of which he pursues justice in order to resemble the Creator in His wisdom and justice?"

To this the rabbi responded: "That which you do express is religion based on speculation and system, the research of thought, but open to many doubts. Now ask the philosophers, and you will find that they do not agree on one action or on one principle, since some doctrines can be established by arguments, which are only partially satisfactory, and still much less capable of being proved."

The conversation continued and the rabbi later offered a parable. If you were told that the king of India was a great man, just, admirable, virtuous, and a wonderful leader of his people, would this information cause you to revere him? The answer must be no, since you cannot judge the truth of these statements in the abstract. However, if the king sent you gifts which reflected his wisdom and generosity, compassion, etc., would you be able to make a better judgment about him? The answer is yes. So too it is with God. Statements about his attributes are philosophical abstractions, and cannot be verified on their own terms. When we want to know about God, we need to evaluate the gifts He has given us—the universe, the Torah, our lives. From these creations we can proceed to understand aspects of God. It is experience—history—which is the source of our understanding of God. It is our ancestors who have passed down to us their own experiences with God and who have shown us how God has manifested Himself to them in their lives.

It is beyond human ability to describe how God's providence works in every detail. It is not fair to attribute each success or failure, each day of health or illness to a specific decision of God to reward or punish someone. We lack control and understanding of God's providence. God told Moses: "I am that I am." Yet this incomprehensible God has also revealed Himself to human beings through the universe He created; and to Israel, through the Torah which He has given this chosen people.

It is One God Who creates light and darkness, "good and evil." To understand this reality, human reason is inadequate. The truth is to be sought in personal spiritual experience, in profound meditation and calm.

10. | CONFRONTING DEATH

Is Death a Problem?

Living in modern Western culture leads one to the conclusion that death is somehow a problem. It is an evil to be postponed, camouflaged, denied. In its aversion to death, our culture teaches us even to avoid saying that someone has died. Rather, we substitute euphemisms such as "passed away," or "passed on," or "expired."

Since the aging process is identified with the approaching of death, aging is also viewed as a problem. Billions of dollars are spent each year on cosmetics, dyes, medical procedures and other vanities—all in an effort to hide the aging process.

Clearly, death is a problem for our society. Doctors are supposed to cure all our diseases and prolong our lives indefinitely. In some way, death may be seen as a failure of medical science. If only the right drugs could be discovered, if only a new operation could be perfected, if only more research could be financed . . . then, presumably, we would not have to die, or at least not for a very long time.

Elias Canetti, in his book "The Torch in My Ear," has expressed the modern repugnance for death. "The aim is not to parrot the banality that so far all human beings have died: the point is to decide whether to *accept* death willingly or stand up against it. With my indignation against death, I have acquired a right to glory, wealth, misery, and despair of all experience. I have lived in this endless rebellion."[1] This is a point of view which appeals to our sense of heroism, our intellectual existentialism.

Ernest Becker's "The Denial of Death" is built on the modern assumption that death is at the root of human fear and is the underlying motivation of our pattern of behavior. "The human animal is characterized by two great fears that other animals are protected from: the fear of life and the fear of death."[2] Death creates terror within us, and this terror dominates our lives.

Philippe Aries, who has studied the Western attitudes on death over the centuries, notes that in earlier times the terror of death was not so pronounced as it is now. In fact, he suggests that the oldest kind of death is the "tame death," the death that is accepted in a fairly natural, non-fearful way. "It has by now been so obliterated from our culture that it is hard for us to imagine or understand it. The ancient attitude in which death is close and familiar yet diminished and desensitized is too different from our own view, in which it is so terrifying that we no longer dare say its name."[3]

For moderns in the Western world, although we may verbalize that death is natural and normal, we rebel against this knowledge. We idealize heroes who defy death or who scorn death: even if they themselves die in the process. This is one of the ironies of human existence: life is an obstacle course which, if we run it very successfully, we will die of old age.

Death Defiance

Franz Borkenau has charaterized cultures as death denying (such as modern America), death accepting (such as Eastern civilizations), or death defying (such as among warlike peoples).[4] Obviously, cultures contain elements of all these characterizations and can never be neatly confined to the definitions of psychologists and anthropologists. Yet, these are useful categories which generalize dominant tendencies within societies.

Rabbi Maurice Lamm, author of "The Jewish Way in Death and Mourning," gave a lecture in which he described the Jewish attitude as being death defying.[5] Jewish tradition has emphasized the sanctity of life, the obligation to preserve life even when it entails violating halakhah. One may desecrate the Sabbath to save a life; one may eat forbidden food if that is the only way to save his life. The intent of halakhah is clearly to support life and to preserve its sanctity. When life is endangered, the halakhah is to violate halakhah if that can lead to the saving of the person's life. In its desire to defy death, Jewish tradition does everything possible to insure a continuance of life.

The Jewish attitude is reflected in the confession which one is supposed to recite before he dies. The Shulhan Arukh (Y.D. 338:2) records the text of the confession: "I admit before You, God, my God and God of my ancestors, that my cure and my death are in Your hands. May it be Your will that You heal me with a complete healing. And if I die, may my death be an atonement for the sins, transgressions and violations which I have sinned, transgressed and violated before You. And place my portion in the Garden of Eden, and let me merit the world to come reserved for the righteous." The confession indicates a tenacity to life. Even when it appears obvious that one will die, he first asks God to heal him. Only then does the individual consider the eventuality of his death. The confession is conditional, not admitting the inevitability of death.

Jewish legal sources emphasize the responsibility of helping the ill person in his battle against death. For example, the Shulhan Arukh (Y.D. 337) rules that it is forbidden to tell a seriously ill person of the death of one of his close relatives. Such news could break his heart and reduce his ability to resist his sickness. Even if a relative died over whom the ill person is obligated to mourn, we are still not to inform him of the death, nor tear his garments, nor cry, nor eulogize in his presence. Rabbi Yoel Sirkes, in his commentary known as the Bah, comments that we should not even inform an ill person of the death of someone who is not related to him. By mentioning someone else's death and by displaying our sadness, the ill person may become frightened and disheartened.

When informing a dying person of his obligation to recite the confesison, we must do so in a cautious and gentle way. The halakhah provides a formula: "Many have confessed but have not died; and many who have not confessed have died. And many who are walking outside in the marketplace confess. By the merit of your confessing, you live. And all who confess have a place in the world to come." Rabbi Sirkes suggests that an ill person should not be told to confess unless he is obviously in the process of dying. But if he is not yet at that last stage, he should not be told to confess, even in a gentle fashion, since this would break his heart and make him give up his fight for life.

The reverence for life over death is also evident in the laws concerning a *goses*, a dying person in the last hours of life. The halakhah prescribes that a *goses* should not be moved, since even the slightest disturbance might cause him to die. Someone who does move a *goses* is equated with one who has shed blood. The message is emphatic: death must not be hastened; life is sacred.

The Jewish laws of mourning seem to view death as a defeat. Mourners tear their garments, and for seven days they sit on the floor, refrain from shaving, from wearing new or cleaned clothes. They do not wear leather shoes, and they avoid social conversational amenities. These are all signs that death is bad; that death is stronger than life. Death angers and frustrates us.

Jewish defiance of death is illustrated by some prophetic verses which are recited during the mourning period. Drawing on the words of Isaiah, we console the mourners by saying that God "will utterly destroy death forever; and the Lord God will wipe the tear from every face. . . . Your dead shall live again, the mortal being shall rise up; awake and sing joyously, you who dwell in the dust, for as the reviving dew on grass shall be your dew, when earth shall bring forth her dead." Ultimately, then, death will itself be defeated by God, and life will prevail. Belief in the resurrection of the dead and in the "destruction" of death certainly contribute to the idea that Jewish culture is death defying.

Death Acceptance in Jewish Tradition

It is inaccurate, however, to define Judaism as being a death defying culture. There are also strong elements—even dominant elements—which show Judaism to be accepting of death. Too seldom is attention given to the death accepting aspect of Jewish religious culture.

Which of the Biblical heroes in the Torah expresses a fear or dislike of death? Where do our Biblical ancestors express a defiance of death? The fact is that they lived quite at ease with the idea of dying. The Torah relates that when Abraham died he was old and satisfied, that he was gathered unto his ancestors. On reading about Abraham's death, we are not saddened, nor do we feel that Abraham himself was sad. Rabbi Mosheh ben Nahman, an outstanding Biblical commentator of medieval Spain, noted about Abraham's death that God shows the righteous people the reward they will receive in the world to come.[6] This information satisfies the righteous as they are dying. This means that the righteous, such as Abraham, do not resist their impending death; they welcome it.

This pattern continues throughout the Torah. When Isaac was old and expected to die, he planned to give his blessing to his son. When Jacob neared death, he called Joseph to ask him to arrange his burial in the land of Canaan. He then gave his blessing to his grandsons, and also left his last words to his children. Isaac and Jacob seem to have accepted the reality of death and tried to put their houses in order before dying. There is no evidence of death defiance.

Before Joseph died, he candidly told his brothers that his

end was near. He told them that God would one day lead the children of Israel back to the promised land. He also left instructions that his bones should be brought out from Egypt when the Israelites ultimately returned to their own land.

The Torah offers a description of the death of Aaron the High Priest. God informed Moses and Aaron that Aaron would be gathered unto his people (Numbers 20:22–29). Aaron's priestly garments were removed and given to his son Elazar. A midrash teaches that Moses did not inform the Israelites of Aaron's approaching death.[7] He feared that— since they loved Aaron so much—they would pray to God to spare Aaron's life, attempting to prevent God's decree from being fulfilled. But this would be contrary to God's wise plan; Aaron was supposed to die. Death was not an evil for the person who died.

Even the death of Moses is consistent with the pattern of death acceptance. Moses did not ask for immortality, only for the privilege of living long enough to enter the promised land. The tragic quality of Moses' demise is not due to the fact that he died; but that he died without having fulfilled his goal.

Accepting death as the natural end of life does not imply that life is unimportant or not worth preserving and extending. Biblical characters accepted the reality of death, but did not want to die violently or prematurely. Cain, Lot and Jacob all expressed the fear of dying in an unexpected or violent way. But this does not mean that they defied death once their natural end had come.

There are many evidences in rabbinic literature which also reflect death acceptance. A midrash informs us that when Sarah died, Abraham and all the people of the land mourned for her. The weeping and lamenting were so universal that Abraham himself had to offer consolation to others. "My children," he said, "take not the death of Sarah too much to heart. There is one event unto all, to the pious and impious alike. I pray you now, give me a burying place with you, not as a gift but for money."[8] Philo (*De Abrahamo*, 44) wrote that Abraham mourned only a short time for Sarah, since immoderate mourning would be unfitting for a wise person, who should not feel sorry when restoring to God the deposit entrusted to Him.

The same idea finds expression in the story of the students of Rabbi Yohanan ben Zaccai, who came to console their master on the death of his son (*Avot de Rabbi Natan*, chapter 14). Only Rabbi Eliezer ben Arakh gave proper consolation. He said: "I will give you a parable to what the matter should be compared: to a man who was given an object to watch by the King. Each day he would cry and scream. He would say: 'Woe unto me! When will I peacefully be free of this object?' So it is with you, Rabbi. You had a son who learned Torah, prophets and writings, mishnah, halakhot, aggadot, and he has been freed from this world without sin. Shall you receive consolations when you have returned intact the object entrusted to you?"

The Talmud (Berakhot 10a) reports that King David sang a special song (*shirah*) five times: in his mother's womb; when he was born and saw the stars; when he was nursed by his mother; when he saw the wicked destroyed. Finally, he sang a song when he considered the day of death. What song did he sing? "Barekhi nafshi," bless the Lord, O my soul. Lord my God, you are very great, you are robed with glory and majesty.

A striking midrash (*Eliyahu Rabba*, 16, 81) remarks that the day of Adam's death was celebrated by his descendants as a festival. They rejoiced that man is mortal, for otherwise he would not do the will of his heavenly Father. Death is not accepted with passive resignation, but with song and festivity.

That death is considered to be an actual good is reflected in the midrash on Genesis 1:31. The Torah states that when God finished creating the world, He looked at it and declared it to be very good. The midrash (*Bereshit Rabba*) interprets the words "hineh tov me'od" (behold it was very good) as referring to death. That is, God examined His creation, realized that death was a feature of it, and declared that the creation was excellent. Without death, the world would be imperfect.

The ultimate meaning of human life is inextricably bound to the fact that humans die. Mortality provides life with intensity, deep emotion and profundity. To deny or to defy death is to deny or defy a primary source of life's meaning.

Rabbi David Ibn Zimra, one of the great Sephardic rabbis of the 16th century, considered the following question: how could Adam have followed Eve's advice to sin after he had been so well treated by God?[9] He answered: It is well understood that everything ultimately returns to its origin. This is true of all living things including humans. Adam knew this. When God commanded Adam not to eat from the tree of knowledge of good and evil, He threatened the punishment of death. This referred to an essential death, not a natural death. Adam realized that his natural death was inevitable; he did not believe himself to be immortal. Adam knew that there was a tree of life in the Garden of Eden but did not know where it was. The snake's argument to Eve, later conveyed by Eve to Adam, was that if they ate from the tree of knowledge of good and evil, they would be like God in their knowledge and understanding. Adam believed that if he ate from the tree of knowledge he would learn where the tree of life was. He could then eat from it and serve God eternally, without fear of death. He reasoned that it would be satisfactory to transgress one of God's commandments in order to gain the privilege of serving God forever. This explains Adam's motive for violating God's commandment. But he was punished because his premise was wrong. God did not want him, or other humans, to be immortal like the angels. He wanted death to be part of the human condition.

A death defying culture is troubled by death. A death

accepting culture is at ease with the idea of dying. The Jewish tradition is a balance between these two types of culture. The death defying elements of Judaism heighten concern for the value of life. The death accepting aspects teach one to face death with wisdom and realism. Understanding how to die gives us understanding on how to live.

The Talmud (Berakhot 17a) records a statement by Rabbi Yohanan who, when finishing his study of the book of Job, said: "The end of a human is to die and the end of an animal is to be slaughtered and everything stands ready for death. Happy is the one who was raised in the Torah and whose involvement was in the Torah; he brings pleasure to his Creator. He was raised with a good name and he died with a good name from this world. About such a one, Solomon said: 'Better is a name than precious oil, and the day of death than the day of birth.'" Rabbi Yohanan offers a classic Jewish perspective on death and life. Death is natural and inevitable; but this does not mean that life is merely a dream, an illusion without meaning. Rather, one should live a life dedicated to Torah, and earn a good name. The day of death is better than the day of birth in the sense that the struggle through life has been completed. Looking back at a total life, it is possible to evaluate if it was lived well, in accordance with the teachings of the Torah. Death is accepted with wisdom, not despair.

Death from the Perspective of the One Who is Dying

Discussing and contemplating death as "outsiders" is different from dealing with death while actually undergoing the experience of dying. There is important wisdom to be culled from those who face death experientially, not merely as an intellectual abstraction.

Dr. Elisabeth Kubler-Ross, in her research with terminally ill people, has concluded that the dying person passes through different stages in dealing with his illness and ultimate death.[10] He may deny the fact that he is ill; he may visit one doctor after another hoping for a favorable diagnosis. He may hide the fact of his illness from friends and family. A dying patient will enter a stage of anger: Why me? He may bargain with God for an extension of life, promising to be a better person if only he recovers. Then, he will try to put his house in order—make sure his will is drawn, that all unfinished business is settled.

When a person realizes that he is really dying, he may sink into a state of depression. He begins to mourn himself on his impending death. He may withdraw into silence, showing little interest in those who visit him. Finally, once having passed through these stages, he will arrive at acceptance of death. At this stage, he is beyond grief and sorrow, beyond his own depression and sadness. With acceptance, the person has reached the point where he is ready to die, even wants to die.

This point of acceptance is a pleasing climax to life. One has attained life's most profound wisdom; he sees life for what it is, without illusion or delusion.

The thoughtful scientist, Lewis Thomas, has written: "We may be about to rediscover that dying is not such a bad thing to do after all. Sir William Osler took this view: he disapproved of people who spoke of the agony of death, maintaining that there was no such thing." Drawing on the research on people who seemed to die but then were resuscitated, Thomas notes that "those who remember parts or all of their episodes do not recall any fear or anguish. Several people who remained conscious throughout, while appearing to have been quite dead, could only describe a remarkable sensation of detachment."[11]

A Jewish perspective on the experience of death is offered by Rabbi Hayyim David Halevy, currently Sephardic Chief Rabbi of Tel-Aviv.[12] Drawing on recent scientific research as well as on Jewish mystical texts which describe the experience of death, Rabbi Halevy concludes that death is actually a marvelous happening. It is filled with light, glory, satisfaction. Interviews by psychologists of people who have seemingly died but then "returned" to life indicate that these individuals experienced death uniformly as a wonderful thing.

Death, then, is not experienced by the dying person as something bad. If a person is ready for death, it is probably a beautiful event. A Talmudic aphorism (Ketubot 103b) teaches: "One who dies from the midst of laughter—this is a good sign for him. One who dies from the midst of crying—this is a bad sign for him." Death acceptance brings a happy death. Death resistance brings tears and suffering.

Reaching a level of death acceptance may be the most profound experience a person can have in his entire life. He can view his life from the perspective of one who is about to leave this world. One who is dying, and who accepts this reality, may attain new insight and understanding; it is as though he receives the key to solving the riddle of life. One who attains death acceptance before dying is imbued with serenity, wisdom, love.

Considering death from the perspective of the dying leads to an appreciation of the wisdom of Jewish tradition which views death as tov me'od, very good. Since we value life, life should be respected and maintained. But since we also value death, it should be accepted when it comes.

The Talmud (Tamid 32a) records some questions which Alexander of Macedon asked to a group of rabbis. Two of the questions and the rabbis' responses are: Question: What should a person do in order to live? Answer: He should make himself die. Question: What should a person do in order to die? Answer: He should make himself live.

This enigmatic dialogue might be understood as follows. What should a person do in order to live? He should make himself aware of his own impending death, imagine himself to be dying. In this way, he will appreciate the value of every moment of life. He will see things with an intensity and love which can only be experienced by someone who appreciates that he is about to lose something precious. In other words, in order to live meaningfully, one must recognize his mortality.

What should a person do in order to die? He should make himself live. He should live his life fully, without fear of death. He should avoid becoming melancholy over the reality of death. If one gives himself fully to life, he can give himself fully to death when the time comes.

Mourning

If death is good and is to be accepted as a positive feature of God's creation, why do we mourn our dead? Why are funerals so somber? Why is death associated with crying, wailing and lamenting?

These questions return us to the balance which the Jewish tradition strikes between death defiance and death acceptance. So much emphasis is placed on life, that death is not easy to accept. Yet, wisdom is to accept death. Rabbi Yaacov (Pirkei Avot 4:22) taught: "Better is one hour in penitence and good deeds in this world than all the life of the world to come; but better is one hour of spiritual repose in the world to come than all the life of this world." There is an ambivalence, a recognition of the balancing values of life and death.

Philosophically speaking, we probably should not mourn for our dead. In fact, we probably do not mourn for them even when we think we do. According to Jewish tradition, the soul is immortal. A person who has died—certainly a good person—will receive magnificent rewards from God in the world to come. Moreover, the one who has died is now free from all the turmoil, pain and confusion of this world. No, we do not cry for the one who has died. We cry for ourselves. We mourn because we will miss the presence of the loved one who has died. We feel lonely, deprived, even guilty for our bad behavior towards the deceased. We mourn because we feel sorry for ourselves. These are legitimate feelings.

Even though we might affirm philosophically that death is a positive feature of creation, we are still pained by the loss of a loved one. Philosophy is one thing, emotional reaction is quite another thing. And both elements must balance each other. Jewish tradition requires us to mourn our near relatives—even if we have philosophically accepted death. But Jewish tradition forbids us from mourning over much—since we must recognize death as part of God's design.

The Jewish laws of mourning balance emotionalism and philosophical wisdom. Mourners are supposed to cry and are expected to participate in burying the dead. There is no camouflage of death, no attempt to deny the starkness of what has happened. Mourners tear their garments, sit on the floor for seven days, and—in a sense—withdraw from their normal social context of life. They are free to be angry, upset, guilt-ridden. But mourning is not just a private matter. During the seven day mourning period, friends and relatives visit the mourners and offer consolation. In fact, the mourners, who ostensibly want privacy in order to grieve over their loss, are placed into an active social setting. They see friends and relatives whom they may not have seen for a long time. People come with kind words, gifts of food, messages from friends from out of town. Even as the mourners feel the desire to be alone in their sadness, they also feel drawn to the well-wishers who come to share the experience with them.

The blend of Jewish wisdom and Jewish realism is apparent in a Talmudic discussion (Berakhot 46b) which deals with the question: what should people say when they come to a house of mourning? The opinion of the sages is that they should say a blessing, "barukh hatov vehameitiv," blessed is God Who is good and Who does good. Rabbi Akiba disagrees, saying that they should recite the blessing, "barukh dayyan ha-emet," blessed be the true Judge. The opinion of the sages seems to be that death must be accepted as a positive good; therefore, we recite a blessing praising God's goodness when visiting a house of mourning. Rabbi Akiba, on the other hand, suggests a blessing which expresses resignation in the face of death. The Talmudic discussion concludes that both blessings are to be recited. In fact, the themes of both blessings are incorporated in the blessing following the mourner's meal after a funeral. The text is: "You are good and You do what is good. You are the God of truth and Your decree is just. You take back our souls in Your universal rule, doing according to Your will, and we are Your people, Your servants. Whatever befalls, we must acknowledge You and bless You." After making these statements recognizing God's goodness and justness, the text goes on: "May He Who gives strength to the bereaved, in His compassion give solace in this bereavement to us and all His people Israel." The claim of the grieving heart in need of consolation is balanced with the claim of the wise mind which accepts death.

Death is not an evil. It is a natural event which occurs to every living being.

Death is not the opposite of life. Rather, life and death are interrelated parts of a continuum of existence, an eternal rhythm. A philosophy of death and a philosophy of life are not separable. Jewish tradition, in its balance of death defiance and death acceptance, puts both life and death in perspective.

11. | THE NATION OF ISRAEL

Why should so many people over so many centuries have desired to destroy the Jews? Why should anyone have cared about a small number of people who observed their own religion quietly and peacefully? Why, even today, do the nations of the world devote so much time and energy to criticizing, attacking, and calling for the extermination of the Jewish state—which has a total Jewish population of three and a half million out of the world population of over four billion? Why do the nations of the world begrudge the Jewish people one tiny bit of land known as Israel, when the land of Israel occupies an infinitesimal amount of the territory of the earth? It makes no sense at all. And yet it is so. Apparently, the very existence of the Jewish people and of Israel represents a serious challenge to other peoples. They recognize that Israel's existence is indeed a miracle, but they do not want to admit this obvious fact. The very existence of the Jewish people is a thorn in the side of religions which claim to have superceded the religion of Israel, and to nations which reject the religious foundation which Israel has given to much of our civilization.

The historian, Fernand Braudel, has noted that in spite of the ability of the Jewish people to adapt to many societies and situations over the centuries, they have maintained their "basic personality." The Jewish people have threaded their way through history and—against enormous odds—have

149

not lost themselves in the process. The destiny of Israel, its strength, its survival and its misfortunes are all the consequence of its remaining irreducible, refusing to be diluted, that is, of being "a civilization faithful to itself."[1]

The Torah and religious traditions of Israel have served to keep the Jews united in spirit, even when divided into communities through the world. Halakhah, Jewish law, has been a powerful influence for maintaining similarities in Jewish observances and practices wherever Jews lived. The Jewish people, even in exile, always viewed themselves as part of the nation of Israel. The Torah and religious traditions were major components of the Jewish nation. Though living in exile for many centuries, the Jews never lost sight of the fact that they intended to return to their homeland in Israel. Their prayer books were filled with dreams of return. Wherever they lived, they viewed themselves as part of a Jewish nation in exile. They governed themselves according to their own laws. Although they conformed to the laws and customs of the societies in which they lived, the Jews remained tenaciously faithful to their own way of life. Jewish communities have always had their own rabbinic courts, religious schools, communal institutions, communal government. The Jews formed themselves into *kehillot*, communities, and to the extent possible, they governed themselves. This was true of all Jewish communities until modern times.

Western civilization offered a serious challenge to Jewish nationhood by offering "emancipation." Being allowed to leave their ghettos and to attend Western schools, to become citizens of the countries in which they lived, to participate fully in the cultural, spiritual and economic life of their societies—many Jews were lured to the opportunities offered by the new openings. Emancipation brought many advantages to individual Jews, but posed serious threats to Jewish nationhood. Jews in Germany and elsewhere in Europe assimilated so quickly, that many of them defected from Jewishness altogether—converting to the dominant Christian faith. Jewish religious observances struck "enlightened" Jews as being archaic. A literature sprouted up among the Jews which reflected the tremendous turmoil within the community. On one side were the "progressive" reformers; and on the other, were the impenetrable traditionalists who feared making any accommodation to the non-Jewish world. The first group preferred to assimilate, while the latter group preferred to remain in ghettos. This intellectual struggle has characterized Jewish life since the late 18th century to our own time. The emergence of a political Zionist movement in the 19th century, and the establishment of the State of Israel in 1948, have helped strengthen the Jewish notion of its own nationalism—but, interestingly, the conflict of the enlightenment continues to trouble Jews even now. There are still those who prefer to think of Judaism as distinct from Jewish nationalism. This dichotomy is essentially a reaction to emancipation, and is not the classic, normative Jewish position.

Rabbi Eliyahu Benamozeg, in his book *In Ethical Paths*, offers a comparison between Christian ethics and Jewish ethics. Benamozeg notes that the Jewish tradition encompasses two different aspects: the national *(mediniyut)* and the ethical *(musar)*. Jewish nationalism and Jewish ethics are intertwined and therefore, at first glance, seem to be less elevated than Christian ethics. But in reality, Christian ethics are not applicable to national life. They speak of humility, suffering, compassion etc. Yet which nation on earth will allow itself to be attacked and not defend itself? Which will forgive debts or insults or cruelties against its people? In contrast, Jewish tradition is realistic in linking ethical teachings with national and practical concerns. The Torah is not merely a document which outlines the religion of Israel, but is also the national covenant between Israel and God.[2]

Rabbi Benzion Uziel was one of the important religious thinkers of the 20th century. He devoted much thought to explaining Jewishness—both in its religious and national dimensions. For example, he offered an interpretation of the traditional three weeks of mourning which are observed by Jewish people between the Hebrew dates of Tammuz 17 and Ab 9. Both of those dates are fast days in commemoration of the siege and destruction of Jerusalem in ancient times. Rabbi Uziel argues that the purpose of these weeks of national mourning is to seek the underlying reasons for the destruction of our national structure in antiquity. "Jewish mourning is not merely mourning over something lost which never returns; such mourning is an empty and vain task. What good is mourning for something which is lost and which will never return? Rather, our mourning on these days aims at clarifying the significance of our loss, and the lack within us created by our national destruction; and to search for ways to restore that which has been lost, to build that which has been destroyed, and to restore the ruins. And so our rabbis taught: all who mourn Jerusalem will merit to see its rejoicing."

According to Rabbi Uziel, the national structure depends on three things. First, there must be a recognition of a national charter and a belief in the ability to achieve its goals. Second, there must be unified action towards fulfilling this charter. Third, there must be a homeland and independent state which is the place in which the national charter can be fulfilled. The first responsibility of a nation is to know itself. " . . . An awareness of the charter in its clarity, and a belief in achieving it—these form the essential foundation upon which the entire national structure rests and sustains itself forever."[3]

It is vital, therefore, for Jews to be deeply aware of their own national character. "An uncertain faith or an erroneous faith is a fire which eats the foundations and a worm which gnaws at its soul." Those who lack this faith and commitment live without purpose. They do not work for the sake of the goal but only for their own pleasure, to gain honor or money.

Rabbi Uziel states that Israel in its relation to the nations is like a prophet in his relationship to the people. A prophet is one who received a message from God. He may not want to be a prophet, but he has no option. Once he understands clearly the meaning of the message he has received, he has no choice but to deliver it, and to try to shape his life and their lives accordingly. Likewise, Israel must understand its own divine message and must live according to it. This is the precise strength and greatness of Israel. When the Jews doubt or do not understand their own specific mission, they stumble and fall.

A nation does not exist on ideas alone, but needs specific actions. Spiritual uplift is not enough. Studying, praying, and thinking must be supplemented by deeds. National ideals are empty unless they are attached to behavior, unless they influence the way people live. "The good deeds to which the spirit of a nation gives birth—these are the mirror through which one can see the soul of the nation . . . " During the last period of the Second Temple, under the Romans, Jewish beliefs were strong, but their religious actions were weakened. "Although we did not follow the gods of Rome, yet the ways of Rome and its people, its laws and statutes, entered into our land; and in this way our unity was destroyed and our strength was sapped." Not living by our own distinctive way of life leads to our own destruction. Following the ways of others reduces us. Without our even realizing what is happening to us, assimilation into other cultures robs us of our own identity.

Rabbi Uziel draws a lesson from the Sabbath.[4] The commandments for the Sabbath are *zakhor*, remember, and *shamor*, observe. The two go together like a flame and an ember. It is not enough to think of the philosophy and to remember the meaning of the Sabbath, but one also must perform specific activities in observance of the Sabbath. It is necessary to tie the ideals to a real world of action. He criticizes those who violate the laws of Shabbat, since they undermine a basic element of Jewish nationhood. "Individual freedom is limited by national foundations and principles." Since the

Sabbath is intrinsic to the nationhood of Israel, any Jew who violates it is threatening the well-being of the entire people. "Individual freedom is limited by public consent *(da-at ha-tsibur)*." The importance of a Jewish community, and of the Jewish state, is to provide the social and political context for the realization of Jewish religious ideals. A Jewish community or Jewish state which abandons its own spiritual heritage in order to follow the ways of other peoples is selling itself out.

Rabbi Uziel speaks of two kinds of gatherings.[5] One is a gathering in a specific place where people come together for a united purpose. The second kind of gathering is a spiritual one, a uniting around an encompassing idea or thought. The individual communities of Jews in all the lands of the dispersion and even in Israel are known as holy congregations *(kahal kadosh)*. Each *kahal* exists individually, but all stem from and are nurtured by the ideas which gather them together into one greater *kahal*, the Jewish people. It is the ideas and values of the Torah which serve as the unifying and unique agents for the people of Israel. The political leader of Israel must have the power not only to gather the people to one place or to one political goal, but must also be able to relate to the spiritual life of Israel, to unite them in their commitments to the Torah.

In explaining the mystery of Jewish survival, Rabbi Uziel has argued: "In every place where Israel was exiled, they carried with them first and foremost their scrolls of the Torah. They built holy arks for them, and made sanctuaries for prayer and gathering. They established yeshivot and schools to study Torah. Over all, they established a kingdom deep within themselves, in the form of rabbis and leaders of congregations. . . . "[6] The unique national feature of Israel has been this sense of transcendent unity, a commitment to the spiritual ideas of the Torah, the commitment to Jewish values and observances even when these entailed personal sacrifice.

Rabbi Uziel has taught, therefore, that the Torah provides meaning to Jewish peoplehood. Jews who do not understand or do not observe the teachings of the Torah contribute to a weakening of the entire Jewish people. Just as a prophet needed to understand God's messge before he could communicate it to others, so the people of Israel must understand its own charter—the Torah—before it can properly express its own identity to others. Jewish peoplehood is based on divine revelation. That revelation created not just a religion, but a nation.

Conversion to the Jewish People

The Jewish people has a national and religious identity. It is an error to think of Judaism as a faith, similar to the religious faiths of other religions. Even a Jew who does not have "faith" remains a Jew, part of the Jewish nation. But the Jewish nation is founded on a divine revelation. The religious and national character of the Jews are inextricably intertwined.

Perhaps the best way to understand what is entailed by the religion-nationhood of Israel is to consider the question of conversion. How can a non-Jew join the people of Israel? What exactly must he/she accept? What does the convert convert to: a religion or a nation or both?

Gerut, conversion to the Jewish people, has become one of the most controversial issues confronting modern Jews.[7] The Jewish people has always welcomed sincere converts who wish to become part of the nation and religion of Israel and who willingly accept the responsibility of observing the commandments. However, in our times, many (perhaps most) candidates for conversion are not motivated by an objective love and commitment to Judaism or to the Jewish people. Rather, they are non-Jews who wish to marry Jewish partners, or who are already married to Jews and now wish to convert for the sake of their children. Often enough, the candidates for conversion are not seriously interested in accepting the observance of all mitzvot and may even so indicate. Sometimes it is clear to the rabbis involved that the would-be convert will not in the immediate future be an observant Jew.

Rabbinic opinion has varied widely concerning conversions which have been motivated by sociological rather than theological considerations. Rabbi Abraham Isaac Kook insisted that only converts who agreed to be fully observant of Jewish commandments should be accepted. If a convert does not observe Jewish religious laws, then the conversion is not really proper. Moreover, those rabbis who accepted such a convert are blameworthy. In one case, Rabbi Kook ruled that a non-Jewish woman who converted for the sake of marriage and clearly had no religious dedication to the traditions of the Torah remains a non-Jew. The conversion ritual was meaningless. "And happy is the one who stands at the breach to guard the purity of Israel, may a blessing of good come to him."[8]

On the other hand, Rabbi Benzion Uziel argued that not only may we accept such converts, but it is actually a positive commandment to do so if we believe the conversion will help create a Jewish home. Even if we surmise that the convert will not be fully observant of our religious traditions, we should perform the conversion in order to prevent intermarriage or loss of children from the Jewish fold.[9]

Between these two positions, there is a wide variety of intermediate opinion. Since this issue is concerned with the very definition of Jewishness, it has evoked deep emotional reactions. This is not a debate on an abstract point of Jewish law: it touches the source of Jewish existence.

In contemporary Jewish life, the term *giyyur kahalakhah*, a conversion according to Jewish law, has become something of a battle cry. Among Orthodox Jews, any conversion which is not done in accordance with traditional Jewish law is an attack on the integrity of the Jewish people. Conversions performed by non-Orthodox rabbis are generally regarded as being invalid. On the other hand, non-Orthodox spokesmen claim that the Orthodox should have no monopoly in determining who is really Jewish, who is an acceptable convert.

Debates on this topic have frightening implications. What is needed now is a fresh look at the primary sources dealing with conversion. We must begin at the beginning— with a definition of what makes a person Jewish.

Going back to the Bible, we find no specific mention of a formal procedure for conversion. Various non-Israelites had attached themselves to the people of Israel, e.g. the mixed multitude who joined the exodus from Egypt. Many laws are stated in the Torah on behalf of the ger, the non-Israelite stranger who lived among the Israelites in the land of Israel; but the Biblical term ger does not seem to mean a full-fledged convert in the modern sense. In II Kings 17:32–3 and in Esther 8:17 we find additional references to groups who in some way attached themselves to the people of Israel. But there is no clear statement describing a conversion procedure.

The classic Biblical example of a righteous convert is Ruth. She tells her Jewish mother-in-law: "Wherever you go, I shall go; and where you lodge, I shall lodge. Your people will be my people and your God will be my God." Ruth has served as a prototype of the ideal convert, one who accepts the Jewish people and religion sincerely and completely. Yet the details of the conversion process of Ruth are omitted from the text.

Yehezkel Kaufman has described Biblical conversion as *giyyur ha-artsi—ha-tarbuti*, a non-Israelite's acculturation into the dominant Israelite culture.[10] Non-Israelites living in the Israelite land would naturally become absorbed by the national culture, accepting various social and religious mores in the course of time. Essentially, this was an ethnic conversion in which religion played a part. Kaufman's observation seems fair. Even going back to the case of Ruth, we note that she first identified with the Israelite people and then with the Israelite God.

Who was an Israelite in Biblical times? Anyone who was born into an Israelite family or anyone who attached himself to the people of Israel and became naturalized. The main factor was *Am Yisrael*, the nation or people of Israel. The strictly religious dimension of conversion did not yet exist.

Kaufman asserts that after the Israelites were expelled from their land and lost their national center, a new type of *gerut* came into being—*giyyur haberit*, a conversion based exclusively on religion. A non-Jew now had to convert to Judaism, not to the culture and people of Israel. In Biblical times, the stranger in the land of Israel gradually adopted Israelite patterns of life; in post-exilic times, the stranger could retain his own language and live in his own land and still convert to Judaism. Religion replaced land and nationality as the definition of an Israelite.

Yet, if we consider the Talmudic sources dealing with conversion, we shall find that Kaufman errs. The religion of Israel never replaced the people of Israel as the main element of self-definition. Even in Talmudic times, conversion was seen primarily as an act of joining the Jewish people, becoming part of the Jewish national destiny. A procedure was delineated for the conversion process, the religious dimension was stressed; but, in the final analysis, peoplehood was the main issue.

There are two major Talmudic sources on this subject which bear examination.

I. *Yebamoth 47a-b:*

"Our rabbis taught: if at the present time a person desires to become a proselyte, he is to be addressed as follows: "Why do you come to become a proselyte? Do you know that Israel at the present time is persecuted and oppressed, despised, harassed, and overcome by afflictions? If he replies, 'I know and yet am unworthy,' he is accepted forthwith, and is given instruction in some of the minor and some of the major commandments. . . . He is also told of the punishment for transgression of the commandments. . . . And as he is informed of the punishment for the transgression of the commandments, so is he informed of the reward granted for their fulfillment... He is not, however, to be persuaded or dissuaded too much. If he accepted, he is circumcised forthwith.... As soon as he is healed, arrangements are made for his immediate ablution.... When he comes up after his ablution he is deemed to be an Israelite in all respects.

"In the case of a woman proselyte, women make her sit in the water up to her neck, while two [three] learned men stand outside and give her instruction in some of the minor commandments and some of the major ones."

This passage is noteworthy for several reasons. First, we see that our initial comments to a would-be convert relate to the difficulties of being a member of the Jewish people. We must ascertain that he is willing to share the burdens of our people, to share sincerely in our destiny. Only after we are satisfied on this score do we instruct him "in some of the minor and some of the major commandments." Even when we do give this instruction, it is far from comprehensive, i.e. it does not include all the mitzvot, only some of them.

Moreover, we are not supposed to persuade or dissuade too much, but rather point out the good and the bad aspects and let him judge for himself if conversion is the right choice for him. If he accepts the responsibilities, then he follows the conversion procedure and is accepted as a complete Israelite.

Rabbi Benzion Uziel, considering this source, concludes that it is apparent that we do not ask the candidate for conversion to fulfill the mitzvot, and it is not even necessary for the Beth Din to know that he will fulfill them. The reason for informing him of some of the commandments is simply to give him a chance to change his mind before it is too late. As long as the candidate is aware in general of what our commandments are, the decision to convert is his.

This source indicates, then, that we are concerned about the convert's becoming a member of our people. One might argue that if a non-Jew agreed to observe all our religious commandments but refused to identify as a member of our people, we would reject his conversion. Indeed, Rabbi

Shlomo Goren, former Ashkenazic Chief Rabbi of Israel, has so ruled. Accepting Judaism is not identical with becoming Jewish.[11]

We can analyze this point from a different perspective. A person born of a Jewish mother is Halakhically regarded as a Jew. He may be completely non-observant of our commandments, or an atheist; yet Jewish law always regards him as Jewish. If we think of being Jewish solely in terms of adhering to Judaism, this law is absurd. Obviously, something else is involved, namely peoplehood. A person born of a Jewish mother is biologically part of our people, regardless of his personal feelings or behavior. By being born Jewish, one is linked to Jewish destiny and may never be written off completely. (A parent who disowns a child, or vice versa, does not sever the biological relationship. The relationship is fixed and eternal.) Being Jewish means being part of the Jewish people. Judaism is the religion of our people but it is not the definition of our Jewishness.

II. *Yebamoth 24b:*

"Mishnah: If a man is suspected of [intercourse] . . . with a heathen who subsequently became a proselyte, he must not marry her. If, however, he did marry her, they need not be separated. Gemara: This implies that she may become a proper proselyte. But against this a contradiction is raised. Both a man who became a proselyte for the sake of a woman and a woman who became a proselyte for the sake of a man . . . are not proper proselytes. These are the words of R. Nehemiah, for R. Nehemiah used to say: Neither lion-proselytes nor dream proselytes nor the proselytes of Mordecai and Esther are proper proselytes unless they become converted as at the present time . . . Surely concerning this it was stated that R. Isaac b. Samuel b. Martha said in the name of Rab: the Halakhah is in accordance with the opinion of him who maintained that they are all proper proselytes."

The Talmud is here concerned with people who convert

for ulterior motives—marriage, fear, dreams, etc. Rabbi Nehemiah argues that such conversions are not valid. But his opinion is rejected. The conclusion—and the accepted law—is that such conversions are indeed valid.

What is the basis for this discussion? Rabbi Nehemiah thinks that individuals who do not convert for idealistic theological and philosophical reasons are to be rejected. This opinion makes good sense if we view the conversion process as one in which the non-Jew's primary decision is to accept Judaism. If he wants to be Jewish for practical considerations but does not genuinely have a belief in and commitment to Judaism, then the conversion process is a sham, an empty ceremonial.

But Rabbi Nehemiah's opinion is rejected. One who converts even with ulterior motives is a valid convert. The law can be understood only if we assume that conversion means becoming part of the Jewish people. If a non-Jew chooses to join our ranks he may do so even if he is not accepting Judaism from theological convictions. A non-Jew who wants to marry someone Jewish and to raise Jewish children has opted to become part of our people, even though the commitment to our religion may be less than perfect.

Another Talmudic passage points in the same direction. Rab and Samuel (Shabbat 68a) speak of a proselyte who became converted among the Gentiles and did not even know the fundamental laws of the Sabbath. Rabbi Moshe Feinstein noted that such a convert is valid even if he is still far removed from observing the mitzvot.[12] This proselyte identified with the Jewish people although his knowledge of Judaism was quite defficient.

In fact, there is no Talmudic legal source that would indicate unequivocally that acceptance of all commandments is a prerequisite for conversion. The central concern of Talmudic as well as Biblical times is the proselyte's commitment to the Jewish people.

What does it mean to become part of the Jewish people? How can we measure the commitment of a would-be convert to our people?

Obviously, more than a token or casual commitment to our people is required. To think otherwise is to degrade our people and our history. It is not possible to codify exact guidelines as to what does or does not constitute a genuine commitment to the people of Israel. The final decision in this matter is really left to the rabbis who are involved in each case. Each candidate for conversion has his or her own dynamics, and must be evaluated individually.

Some cases, though, seem clearly to be acceptable. A non-Jewish spouse of a Russian Jew who sacrificed much to migrate to Israel and to join our people is one example. A non-Jewish partner in marriage who wishes to convert in order to raise the children with a Jewish identity is another. Where it can be determined that the non-Jew is sincerely dedicated to sharing our destiny, carrying our burdens, participating in our communal life, there is a good basis for conversion. Certainly, we must make every effort to inform candidates for conversion of the beliefs and principles of Judaism, of our mitzvot and customs. These are basic factors in the life of our people.

In returning to our classic sources in Bible and Talmud, we have arrived at an old but novel understanding of Jewishness. By stressing this view, we can hope to deal more successfully with the contemporary disputes about gerut. Certainly, much rabbinic literature has been created since Talmudic times, and the earlier concept of conversion has been blurred in the process. It is all the more important, then, to go back to our primary sources and look at them objectively.

The Talmudic Halakhic sources are far more open to receiving proselytes to the Jewish people than some who argue strenuously in the name of Halakhah may want to admit. There is certainly ample support to perform conversions for the sake of marriage if the convert has a genuine commitment to the Jewish people—to identify as a Jew, raise children as Jews, settle in Israel, etc.

Israel and the Nations

Israel has always viewed itself as a nation chosen by God: Israel and God entered a covenant, with the Torah being the document describing this covenant. Interestingly, the Torah does not speak of Israel bringing its message to the other peoples of the world. Even the later prophetic idea that Israel should be the "light unto the nations," does not mean that the people of Israel were ever obligated to convert all the people of the world to the Israelite nation/religion.

The Torah is a document describing the relationship between God and Israel. The Israelites are bound to the terms set forth in the Torah, the oral law, and halakhah in general. Other peoples may have their own chosenness, may follow their own paths to God. Rabbinic tradition teaches that there are seven Noahide laws which all human beings must observe, and which form the basis of simple morality and justice in the world. But beyond these elementary laws of decency, Jewish tradition does not teach that non-Jews must become Jews in order to have the "truth." On the contrary, Jewish tradition holds that there is certainly a place in the world to come for righteous non-Jews.

Chosenness, therefore, has been viewed as a private matter between God and Israel. It is neither a sign of superiority nor inferiority—just a simple historical fact. Even in the "end of days," it is not expected that the non-Jews of the world will all convert to become members of the Jewish people/religion. The prophetic belief that in messianic times everyone will recognize the true One God does not mean that everyone will become Jewish. It is possible to have a true notion of the One God, to be a righteous person, and yet not become part of the Jewish nation.

That the Torah is for Israel, not for all the other peoples in the world, should be clear from the Torah itself. God promised Abraham that his descendants would dwell in the Promised Land. Israelite history cannot be understood without reference to the central role that the land of Israel has played and does play in Jewish national/religious life. Since the Israelite nation is attached to the land of Israel, it is obviously bound by these limitations. All the lands of the earth cannot be Israel, and all the peoples of the world cannot be Israelites. There are many roads to God, Israel following its own distinctive way. Those who wish to join Israel are welcomed. But it is not likely, and not expected, that a very high percentage of the world population will do so.

12. | FAMILY, SOCIETY, INDIVIDUAL

In a thoughtful little volume, "Culture and Commitment," Margaret Mead offered a study of the generation gap.[1] She described three different kinds of culture, each with its own strengths and weaknesses; and she tried to understand contemporary life based on her understanding of these cultures.

A postfigurative culture is one in which the past is the guide to the future. Such cultures are generally quite stable and tradition-oriented. They are characterized by veneration of elders. Parents can predict with reasonable accuracy what their children's lives will be like. Children inherit beliefs, mannerisms and ways of thinking from their elders. The postfigurative culture is so stable and tradition-bound, that there are few surprises within it. People are born, they live and they die—all within a relatively predictable pattern.

In a cofigurative culture, the elders have lost their role as guides. Rather, the new generation learns from peers. An example of a cofigurative culture may be found among immigrants to a new land. To children being raised in a new environment, their parents and grandparents represent the old world, the world that they are trying to leave. Children learn from their native-born contemporaries how to live. A gap opens between the generations. The more that elders try to force the old ways on the young, the more the young will rebel.

Margaret Mead suggests that contemporary American society is a prefigurative culture. There has been a radical break with past patterns of culture. Presently, the elders and the youngers are all immigrants in a new world of technology, space exploration, etc. No one can say what life will be like in ten years or fifty years. It changes so fast and so universally that elders and youngers are all in the same predicament. While a gap remains between generations, this gap can be dealt with sympathetically once everyone realizes that a new reality exists. If the elders have lost their authority, so have the younger contemporaries. No one seems to have the correct answers for the future. And so, there is social turmoil.

This analysis of culture, although much simplified, provides a thoughtful framework for considering the nature of human societies. The categories apply, in varying ways, to developments among the Jewish people over the centuries.

At base, the religious culture of the people of Israel has many postfigurative elements. The Torah commands respect for parents in particular, and for elders in general. The leaders of the people are known as "elders." Tradition is venerated; and it is the elders who understand the traditions best, and who are obliged to transmit them to the new generations. The Torah emphasizes responsibility of the elders to teach the youngers. The Haggadah of Passover captures the essential Jewish spirit. It is an elaborate format for the elders to recount the miracles of God when He redeemed the Israelites from slavery in Egypt. The Haggadah describes the responsibility of transmitting the story to children, whether they are wise, wicked, simple, or even if they do not know how to ask. The point is, the elders are obligated to transmit the story; just as the youngers are obligated to learn it.

Historically, laws of honoring parents and teachers have made it very clear to the young generation that it is the elders who have the authority. The codes of Jewish law have included such regulations as the requirement of children to stand when their parents enter the room, not to sit in their parents' chairs, not to contradict their parents, not even to agree with their parents in public—since the opinions of parents do not need the approval of children.

Many customs have arisen throughout the Jewish world which emphasize respect for parents, teachers, and elders. For example, among Sephardic Jews, whenever an older relative or a teacher is called to read from the Torah scroll, all younger relatives and students stand in respect. It has also been customary for children to kiss the hands of their parents and grandparents in order to receive their blessings. Among many Sephardim, children are named after living grandparents. The firstborn son is named after the father's father, the secondborn son after the mother's father; the firstborn daughter after the father's mother; and the secondborn daughter after the mother's mother. The result of this custom has been to have a number of grandchildren carrying the same name as their grandparents. This practice tended to strengthen family ties, as well as to inculcate in the youngsters the fact that they are named after grandparents and are expected to live according to the standards of their elders.

The Jewish people existed within a general postfigurative cultural pattern until the 18th century. And even then, many communities, especially those not in the West, continued their postfigurative cultural patterns well into the 19th, and even 20th century.

A cofigurative culture emerged among the Jews when a feeling developed that their elders no longer represented the "truth." With emancipation, Jews in Western Europe were anxious to become like the non-Jews around them. Many left their ghettos, physically and spiritually. To many, the old ways were viewed as archaic, passive, primitive. The new opportunities of Western society were seen as great blessings. But, as often happens in cofigurative cultures, people soon realized that the substitute culture was shallow and had problems of its own. In cofigurative society, changes occur so quickly that people lose their sense of connecton with a solid past. They may earn more money, have more advanced educational degrees, live in nicer homes—but they are not necessarily happier than their grandparents or great-grandparents were in a postfigurative society. In fact, people in a cofigurative culture may very well be less happy than their less sophisticated ancestors.

Just as Margaret Mead has argued that moderns are now living in a prefigurative culture, the same holds doubly true for the Jewish people. This is clearly a new era for Jews. Emil Fackenheim, in his book *To Mend The World*, has argued that there has been a rupture in Jewish history.[2] The way we face life now is radically different from the way Jews faced life before the Holocaust. We can no longer speak of God with the same meaning as Jews spoke of God before that disaster. While I disagree with Fackenheim's making the Holocaust the central event which ruptured the present from the past for the Jews, I agree that a rupture has indeed occurred. The Holocaust has been one aspect of the rupture. But it was the emergence of the State of Israel which has put the Jewish people into a prefigurative situation. We now have a generation of Jews who cannot remember living in a world without a Jewish state. When young Jews speak of Israel, of Jewish pride, of nationalism—they speak in terms that the elders do not understand in the same way. Things really are not the same. The ghetto Jew, the victim Jew are not acceptable for the young generation, though these patterns were acceptable to the older generations.

The old ideas of the postfigurative culture are inadequate to deal with Jewish life and thought today. Elders telling the youngers the meaning of Jewishness, as though the elders still had their postfigurative authority, is a sad charade. Elders who speak of caution and who fear change represent impossible categories for many members of the younger generation to accept.

There has been a gap between Jewish thought and reality. Traditions are maintained, even when they no longer correspond to the current situation. For example, the wedding ceremony includes a prayer that God should restore the sound of brides and grooms in the streets of Jerusalem. Yet, the sound of brides and grooms *can* be heard among Jews in Jerusalem today! The ritual has not yet adjusted to the new reality.

Rabbi Hayyim David Halevy, Chief Rabbi of Tel Aviv, has written that it is inappropriate for Jews to recite the traditional prayer on the 9th of Av which asks God to console Jerusalem, "the city which is destroyed, humiliated, empty, without its children."[3] Rabbi Halevy points out that it is not proper to say these words since they are no longer true. He has emended the text to read that God should have mercy on Jerusalem which *was* destroyed, humiliated, empty, without her children. For this very small and very reasonable emendation, Rabbi Halevy was criticized sharply by many traditionalists. These are just small examples which demonstrate that not everyone has yet been able to grasp the new situation in which Jews find themselves today.

This is a new era in Jewish life. The old patience and the old axioms are not totally satisfactory. Most Jews no longer live in a stable, postfigurative cultural setting. The more one insists on pretending that everything is the same as it always was, that everything is just a natural progression and development, the more one removes himself from reality.

The old generations and the young generations of Jews are in a prefigurative culture. We are all immigrants in a new world, a world where Israel is a nation, where Jews assert their national and religious identity without fear or apology. While the past provides guidelines, it does not provide all the answers. The elders need to understand the impatience and confidence of the young. The young need to understand the security and patience offered by the old. And we all need to understand clearly that the future is uncertain, that we need to work together, as immigrants in a new era of the Jewish experience. The last several centuries have been turbulent for the Jewish people. Westernization and assimilation have challenged the fabric of Jewish life. The Holocaust wiped out six million Jews—one third of the entire Jewish population of the time—in just several years. The State of Israel has been involved in one war after another just to insure its survival. The physical and spiritual fragmentation within the Jewish community is staggering. The word "Jew" encompasses individuals of vastly different religious, political, social and economic outlooks. Elias Canetti, in *Crowds and Power*, has observed about the Jews: "Fools may tell stories of their sameness everywhere, but anyone who knows them well will be inclined to think that there are more varied types among them than among any other people. The extent of variation between Jews, both in their nature and their appearance, is one of the most extraordinary phenomena there is."[4]

Jews, then, are part of a prefigurative culture in two senses. First, like all other human beings in the modern world, Jews too recognize the unpredictability of the future due to advances in technology. Second, the Jews are in the midst of their own specific prefigurative culture, a new Jewish era, where the future also is unpredictable and uncertain, where there has been a rupture with the past.

And yet, the Torah was given for all generations. It offers guidance and a social structure which can meet the needs of Jews, even when the postfigurative model has been irrevocably altered.

Does life have meaning? Do generations come and go in an eternal rhythm which has some ultimate significance?

Understanding the Context of Life

In Western society, we are raised to respect and value individualism. Our society stresses individual achievement. We are fascinated by stories of people who were raised in poverty but who became fantastically wealthy due to their own hard work, ambition and talent. As a culture, we idolize "stars," individuals who stand out above all others for their excellence in a particular field.

Our society is competitive. Each child learns at an early age that he must outdo his contemporaries if he is to succeed. He is encouraged to make a name for himself, to distinguish himself from the crowd.

Our American cultural heros are rugged individualists who showed courage and took risks. Individual rights and individual freedoms are highly prized features of our society.

Although Jewish tradition respects the individual, its main focus is on family, community and nation. Even individual achievements have been evaluated not by how much the individual has done for himself, but by how much he has done for his family and community. Instead of being a self-centered individualistic culture, Jewish tradition has stressed the importance of the collectivity. This point becomes very clear when we look at the ceremonies connected with the cycle of life.

When a baby boy is born, he is circumcized on the eighth day in order to enter the covenant of Abraham our father. Before the boy has any awareness of his own separate identity, he is made part of a covenant, part of the destiny of the people of Israel. Those present at a circumcision bless the child's parents with the following words: "May it be God's will that as you have been privileged to introduce your son into the covenant, so may you also be privileged to bring him to the Torah, the Commandments, to the marriage canopy, to a life of good deeds; and let us say amen." Significantly, the blessing is not aimed at the child's health, wealth, ability to make great achievements. Rather, the goal for that child is to learn the Torah, to observe the Commandments, to get married, and to continue the cycle of the Jewish people. Following the naming ceremony, a blessing is given to the child asking God to help him attain the life of Torah, Commandments, marriage, good deeds. The expectations of the family, community and people are clearly enunciated.

In the traditional Sephardic naming ceremony for baby girls, the text does wish the baby health, peace and contentment. It goes on to pray that her parents have the merit of seeing her happily married, a radiant mother of children, rich in honor and joy to a ripe old age. The expectation for the girl, then, is to grow up in good health and strength so that she can marry and have children. Again, the overriding concern is for the continuity of the family and of the people. The individual is important as a building block in the structure of the generations.

The wedding ceremony provides further insight into the Jewish attitude on life. When a man betrothes a woman, a blessing is recited praising God who has sanctified Israel with His Commandments, Who has provided laws of marriage. It concludes: "Blessed are You, Lord, Who sanctifies Your people Israel by the rite of the wedding canopy and the consecration of betrothal." It is noteworthy that the blessing makes no particular reference to the man and woman who are entering a marriage relationship. It does not speak to their individual needs or aspirations. Rather, it provides the context of their life: a life of holiness, a life governed by God's Commandments. At the time of betrothal, when a new link is about to be established in the generations of the Jewish people, we stop to reflect, and to bless God for having sanctified his people Israel. Marriage, and the continuity of generations which it implies, is part of God's plan for us.

The marriage ceremony has six blessings, following the blessing over wine. These blessings reflect the traditional Jewish philosophy of life.

"Blessed are You, Lord our God, ruler of the universe, Who has created all for Your glory." This blessing indicates the context of life. God is Master of the universe, and we are grateful to Him for our very existence.

"Blessed are You, Lord our God, ruler of the universe, creator of man." When God decided to populate the earth, he created Adam: one individual. A mishnah in tractate

Sanhedrin (4:5) comments that God created only one person in order to emphasize the significance of each individual. If anyone kills one human being, it is as though he destroys a universe. Each human life has immense value. The marriage ceremony, then, makes reference to the uniqueness of each human being, of each of the marriage partners.

"Blessed are You, Lord our God, ruler of the universe, Who has created man in Your image. In the likeness of that image You did ordain for him woman made from him for perpetual human succession. Blessed are You, Lord, creator of man." This blessing refers to Adam and Eve, both created in the image of God. When God first created Adam, the Torah states that He created Adam as male and female. In a later account, the Torah states that God put Adam to sleep and created woman from one of Adam's bones. One interpretation can be that Adam was originally created with male and female qualities, and was later divided into two different human beings, one being male and one being female. This wedding blessing refers to God's creation of man and woman and their ability to perpetuate the species together. Both male and female are vital to the world.

"May Zion who has been barren rejoice and exult at the speedy joyful regathering of her children within her. Blessed are You, Lord, Who causes Zion to rejoice in her children." This blessing obviously was composed after the Jews had been exiled from their land. The desire to return to the national homeland was so strong, that a blessing was incorporated into the wedding ceremony. Each Jewish couple was reminded of Zion and Jerusalem during their wedding. In fact, we mention the happiness of Zion before making any blessings referring to the bride and groom.

Thus far, the wedding blessings have followed a pattern: 1. Praising God for the creation of everything—giving meaning to existence; 2. For the creation and uniqueness of each individual; 3. For the special relationship of man and woman; 4. For the nation and land of Israel. Only after these blessings, do we turn to the marriage couple directly. The last two blessings praise God as the One Who gives joy to the bride and groom, and Who makes the bride and groom rejoice together. But even in the last blessing—when we refer specifically to the joy of the bride and groom—we also offer a prayer for the restoration of joy and happiness to the cities of Israel and the streets of Jerusalem.

The ceremonies described thus far provide a context for individual life. They emphasize that each individual is part of a greater reality—a people of Israel, a holy nation. The individual is expected to find meaning in his/her life by sharing in the destiny of his/her people.

When we pray for someone who is ill, we ask that he may be healed together with other Israelites who are ill. When we console mourners, we pray that they may be consoled along with all the mourners of Zion and Jerusalem. The tendency to think of the needs of all Israel, rather than of individual needs, is characteristic of the Jewish prayer book in general. Almost all prayers are recited in the plural form. It is considered arrogance and bad manners for an individual to pray only on his own behalf.

These rituals and prayers are a constant reminder to an individual Jew of his connection with his entire people. He is reminded to think of others even before he thinks of his own needs.

Traditionally, the family structure underscored the pre-eminence of the group rather than the individual. Children were named after grandparents or other relatives. They were part of a family tradition. Relatives often lived in the same neighborhood, so that each individual was actually part of a larger extended family. Since Jews were not allowed to travel on the Sabbath, they had to live within walking distance of their synagogue. In this way, Jewish neighborhoods became extensions of the family. The many festivals and observances of Jewish religion created a special feeling when experienced in a larger group. The entire neighborhood was "home," a place filled with love, understanding, extended family relationships.

Individuals within a Jewish community were entitled to respect. Certainly, even in postfigurative Jewish families there was appreciation of individual talent, achievement and dignity. Yet, the individual was expected to use his talents for the benefit of his family and community. Ideally, Jews did not compete with each other, but worked with each other.

Clashes of Culture

Western technological societies are individual-oriented. Since so much of the world's scientific and technological progress has developed in the West, there is a pervasive assumption among Westerners that their culture is superior to others. Peoples of non-Western cultures are thought to be backward, or passive, or less gifted. After all, if they were as smart as we are, why didn't they make all these scientific achievements? Why are their societies still so underdeveloped in comparison to ours?

Non-Western cultures may be viewed as being quaint, endowed with some ancient wisdom, as being superstitious, primitive. But since Westerners are taught to compare and compete, they generally will conclude that the Western world is more advanced, and therefore superior to, the non-Western world.

This attitude finds expression among Jews as well. Most Jews have been strongly influenced by Westernization. The majority of the world's Jewish population lives or originates in North America and Europe. A minority of the Jewish people have lived for centuries in North Africa and Asia. Western Jews have considered these non-Western Jews to be somewhat backward and uncivilized. During the late 19th and early 20th centuries, Western European Jews established schools throughout Turkey, the Middle East and North Africa in order to raise the standards of the hapless Jews in those backwards countries. Indeed, economic, social and educational conditions in those places were very bad by Western standards. The efforts of Western Jews to upgrade the condition of their non-Western co-religionists were noble and praiseworthy.

Yet, few of the Westerners ever stopped to think that the non-Westerners had worthy cultural traits which deserved to be maintained. The cofigurative Jews of the West did not want to leave the postfigurative Jews of the East in tranquility.

Western culture offered obvious advantages: advanced economic life, better "standard of living," more systematic formal education. But in trying to "save" the non-Westerners, the unwritten agenda was to convert them into Westerners. The goal was to make non-Western Jews understand their own deprivation and cultural decadence; then, they would be able to embrace the higher values of Western Jews eagerly.

The Western/Eastern Jewish interrelationship became explosive with the establishment of the State of Israel. In 1948, the majority of Jews in Israel were of Western background. But shortly thereafter, hundreds of thousands of Jews from Africa and Asia poured into the new Jewish state. The immigrants were generally regarded as being backwards, unskilled, without leadership, without money, without technological expertise. The immigrants came from pre-modern, postfigurative cultures, into a modern, technological, Western-oriented culture. The sparks of friction from the early meetings of cultures were painful and agonizing for all the Jewish people. Even now, after several generations, the Western and non-Western Jewish cultures have not fully blended together.

One of the reasons for the tension is that Westerners do not take the time to appreciate seriously the value of the culture of non-Westerners. Because it is not Western, it is assumed to be inferior—or, at best, exotic. Yet, it may be that the original Jewish values of life are best manifested in the non-Western communities, rather than in the Western communities.

The real question any culture must answer is: do the people of this culture have meaning in life? Are they happy? Do their lives make sense to them? Obviously, it is difficult to answer these questions with generalizations. Nevertheless, it can be argued that the non-Western Jews are able to answer these questions with more confidence than Western Jews. Indeed, non-Western peoples, deeply rooted in their own cultures, may be able to answer these questions better than people living in Western cultures.

The characteristic features of the non-Western communities were postfigurative: emphasis on family, stability of the community, rootedness in tradition. People lived their lives with a deep religious sensitivity, understanding that life was created by God for His own glory. There was no need to compete against others, since the ultimate goal was to work for the betterment of all. Did life in this culture have meaning? Very much so. Were people happy? Yes, since they knew that their lives fitted into a family and community context. They were rooted. When they had problems, they had elders with whom they could discuss them. Was everything perfect in these societies? No, not at all. But individuals knew who they were, and what they were part of, and what they were expected to do with their lives.

In Western society, these questions cannot be answered so simply. It is not an accident that psychiatry and psychology were created in the West. People in the West are more likely to be deracinated, alienated, uncertain of the meaning of their lives. They enjoy the thrill of independence and individuality, but lack the stability that comes with a strong, extended family, and an ancient venerated tradition. It is possible for a Westerner to have incredible wealth, to have all the technological devices and comforts at his disposal—and yet be miserable. Western society teaches us constantly to strive—rather than to enjoy what we already have. In spite of all the technology of the West, it cannot be demonstrated that Western culture is superior to non-Western culture in terms of making people happier or making their lives more meaningful. It is possible that non-Westerners might consider Western culture to be inferior to theirs—and in many ways they would be correct.

The point is not to pit Western against non-Western culture. The reality is that we are in a process of blending different cultural backgrounds. This is a prefigurative era in which we need to gain the benefits of the positive elements of Western and non-Western cultures.

Living in a new era, where many of the underpinnings of the past have been removed, creates a sense of uncertainty about the future. Because we live in such a world, it is all the more important that we recognize the wisdom of Jewish tradition—especially in its non-Western manifestation. We have perhaps become too individualistic. It is time now to turn back to the non-Western, traditional viewpoint that stresses the role of family, community and nation. It is wonderful to develop and utilize technology. But when all is said and done, conveniences and computers do not give life meaning. In all our striving, we seldom stop to pause to ask the question: why are we doing this? What are the implications?

The new era of the Jewish people will find us utilizing Western efficiency, organization and technology. But it will also find us placing more value on family, community, tradition. We need individualistic courage; we also need traditional wisdom and calm.

Economic Life

The Torah (Exodus 22:24-26) describes a case where someone lends money to a poor person and takes his garment as pledge. Since the poor person needs the garment to keep him warm at night, the lender is told that he must return it to the borrower each evening. "For that is his only covering, it is his garment for his skin; wherein shall he sleep? And it shall come to pass, when he cries unto Me, that I will hear, for I am gracious." God becomes involved in this relatively simple economic relationship. From an abstract business point of view, one person lends money to another, and takes a pledge. By right, he should hold the pledge until the borrower pays back his debt. But the Torah teaches otherwise. The borrower and the lender are not engaged in a business relationship, but in a human relationship. The lender must return the pledge to the borrower even though this does not make good business sense. Perhaps the borrower will run away and not pay back his debt. Nevertheless, the lender must give back the garment, and God Himself is on the side of the borrower.

This case exemplifies the Torah attitude on economic life. Business is not conducted for its own sake, but for the benefit of all members of the community and society. The goal of economic life is to provide for everyone's needs as best as humanly possible. The Torah is not capitalistic. It is not concerned with wealth for the sake of wealth. It is concerned with the well-being and dignity of the members of society.

The Torah legislation on behalf of the poor and oppressed is well-known. Farmers were obligated to leave portions of their fields unharvested, leaving it for the poor. Lenders were not allowed to charge interest on their loans. Society had an obligation to protect widows and orphans, and all others who were unprotected.

On each seventh year, debts were cancelled. On each fiftieth year, land was returned to the family which originally owned it. The result of these laws was to prevent chronic poverty within families. The younger generations did not inherit an overwhelming burden of debts from the older generations; and a family could always look forward to a definite time when their property—which they may have had to sell in desperation—would be returned to them.

Within Jewish tradition, charity is known as *tsedakah*, righteousness. Charity is not an option, but is a commandment which one must fulfill. Even a poor person who himself lives off the contributions of others is obligated to share his belongings with those who are in need.

The highest form of *tsedakah* is providing employment for someone who is in need. Also, lending money at no interest is especially important. These forms of *tsedakah* do not demean the poor person. They allow him to keep his own dignity. If he can be helped to earn his own living, he keeps his self-respect. If he takes a loan rather than a hand-out, he still retains his honor, feeling that he will eventually be able to pay back his debt. Economic life provides the framework for spiritual life.

Rabbi Benzion Uziel has analyzed the distinctive Jewish approach to economics. The Sabbath serves as an excellent example. For at least one-seventh of our lives we are free from physical labor and servitude. Shabbat teaches us that we are basically free. Some people object that resting from work on Shabbat hinders productivity. But they forget that human beings are supposed to be masters of the natural world and to be free. "Man creates technology and reveals and exploits the powers of nature hidden in all sections of the creation; technology does not rule man and enslave him."[5] Shabbat does not only mean to rest, but to rest in holiness. It is the holiness of the day which sanctifies one's entire life.

Rabbi Uziel notes that the historic Jewish attitude calls on Jews to work. It is viewed as a commandment to work on the six days, just as it is a commandment to rest on the seventh. But the Jewish attitude on work differs from the attitude of other nations. For others, work is an end in itself. Its goal is to increase production, increase wealth, increase technology. But for Jews, labor is a means to an end, not an end in itself. Rabbi Uziel quotes the opinion of Rabbi Levi of the Talmud: "All of the actions of Israel differ from those of the nations of the world: in their plowing, planting, harvesting, winnowing, etc." The laws of the Torah guide and govern all of these activities in one way or another. Rabbi Uziel writes: "There is no work or labor which does have with it a specific law, a great and elevated traditional Torah above the laws of nature and technology. Labor itself is an intellectual and ethical sanctuary which elevates the soul, improves the spirit, and makes the workers into people of kindness, compassion, love, affection for all creations, open-hearted to all that was created in the image of God—by giving gifts to the poor, and attributing holiness and honor to the teachers of the nation and its spiritual leaders. . . ."

Labor involves a relationship between owners and workers. It is based on honesty and trust. The Torah provides laws governing the responsibility and rights of employers and employees. "Just as Torah without work will in the end be void, so also work which does not have with it Torah is not fit to be called by the name work . . . The Torah of Israel is not hidden in the holy Ark in the synagogue, but goes with us in all our steps in all the places we go, enlightening us with its light and sanctifying us with its sanctity . . . You cannot recognize the splendor of the Torah except as it appears in the thoughts and actions of a person and the nation of Israel, and you cannot recognize the form and structure of a Jew except in the Torah of God which is in his heart and the mitzvot of God which are in all his deeds and actions."[6]

Richard Rubenstein in his book *The Age of Triage,* has drawn a candid picture of the way Western society has operated over the centuries.[7] As new methods of production developed, old forms of economic life were obliterated. Increased efficiency and technology have led to the need for less human labor. Rubenstein describes the process of triage, where natural forces or governments themselves eliminate unneeded, unproductive people. This was effected actively by encouraging emigration, or by actual destruction of populations. Triage was also accomplished passively, by eliminating the means of survival of segments of the population, so

that they died of starvation or disease. Thomas Malthus suggested that poor people be moved to swampy unhealthy areas
so that they would catch diseases and die. In this way, society
would be rid of this unproductive group.

The process of triage is exacerbated by the incredible
rush of technology in our own day. Many blue collar workers
suddenly find themselves redundant. The changes have
come so quickly that many workers have been displaced
without much prospect of finding other employment. Lives
are ruined, families are broken—all in the name of economic
progress.

The teachings of the Torah offer a sharp challenge to the
prevailing economic policies of the industrialized nations.
The Torah's first concern is with the well-being of people.
Technology for its own sake is a monster. It is only important
if it can improve the quality of people's lives. If it improves
some people's lives and destroys others, it should be introduced gradually so that as few people as possible are hurt by
the changes. And those who are displaced should never come
to feel that they are redundant. They are also part of our
society and need to be cared for and loved like anyone else.
The value of a person's life is not measured by how produc-
tive he is economically.

Western society relentlessly pursues a policy of rationalization of productivity. It constantly seeks technologies to
produce things faster and more efficiently. We seldom stop to
ask ourselves why we need to produce so much so quickly.
Do people really need so much? And can people wait a little
longer to get what they need?

We are in competition. Each company wants to produce
more goods at a faster rate at lower cost per unit. This is called
efficient productivity, and makes a company competitive.
Nations compete against each other, so even if we decide not
to engage in the race, others would still be doing so. Then we
would "fall behind."

But what is the point of efficiency, productivity, cost per

unit? Can the quality of our lives be measured simply by the gross national product figures? If our companies can produce more clothes than we can wear, more machinery than we can use, more cars than we can drive—why is this considered a sign of a successful economy? What happens to all the lives that have been uprooted in the technological rush?

Obviously, it is not likely that the process of rationalization of productivity will be stopped. Triage seems to be a fact of life in modern society.

But perhaps the Torah perspective on economic life can restore some idealism to modern business. The Torah teaches that technology is created by humans to help humans. It is not important in and of itself. Our goal ought not be how well we compete with others, but how well we provide for all the needs of the people in our own society. Just as we need to work and produce things during the six days of the week, we need to rest in the holiness of Shabbat on the seventh day. And it is Shabbat which explains to us why we work on the six other days.

Modern society tends to focus on quantity. Jewish tradition focuses on quality. Modern society keeps asking: how much? Jewish tradition keeps asking: why?

NOTES

Notes to Chapter One

1. Targum Yerushalmi, Genesis 1:1. See also, Rabbi Benzion Uziel, *Hegyonei Uziel*, vol. 1, Jerusalem, 5713, p. 1.

2. *Mishneh Torah*, "Hilkhot Yesodei Hatorah," 2:2.

3. Bereishit Rabba 1:1. There are a number of rabbinic sources expressing the belief that the Torah predated Creation. Among them are Bereishit Rabba 1:4; Vayikra Rabba 19:1; Pesahim, 54a.

4. Abodah Zarah, 3a.

5. See Solomon Schechter, *Studies In Judaism* (second series), Philadelphia, 1908, p. 297.

6. *The Sacred and the Profane*, New York, 1959, p. 156.

7. *On the Kabbalah and its Symbolism*, New York, 1965, pp. 152-3.

8. See Schechter's article, Appendix A, p. 294.

9. *Abudarham Hashalem*, Jerusalem, 5723, pp. 345-6. For laws and customs relating to the blessing of the moon see Rabbi Hayyim David Halevy, *Mekor Hayyim*, vol. 3, Jerusalem 5743, pp. 181-182; and Rabbi Yaacob Huli, *Me'am Lo'ez* on Genesis 1:19.

10. Solomon Zeitlin, *The Rise and Fall of the Judean State*, Vol. 1, Philadelphia, 1968, pp. 248 f.

11. See *Mekor Hayyim*, vol. 2, chapter 97.

Notes to Chapter Two

1. Alan Watts discusses the differences between Eastern and Western perceptions of reality in his many writings. In particular,

see his books: *The Book*, New York, 1972; *Nature, Man and Woman*, New York, 1970; *Psychotherapy East and West*, New York, 1975; *The Wisdom of Insecurity*, New York, 1951.

2. For a discussion of Rabbi Luria's attitude on words, see Gershom Scholem, *Major Trends in Jewish Mysticism*, New York, 1967, p. 254.

3. *Mashal Venimshal*, Jerusalem, 1913, p. 35b.

Notes to Chapter Three

1. *The Sacred and the Profane*, p. 70.
2. *Ibid.*, p. 88.
3. *Ibid.*, p. 107.
4. *Ibid.*, p. 110.
5. There is a debate in the Talmud whether the universe was created in what we call Tishri or Nissan. The popularly accepted view is that God created the world on Rosh Hashanah. See tractate Rosh Hashanah, 11a.
6. Eliade, p. 78.
7. See Yosef Hayim Yerushalmi, *Zakhor: Jewish History and Jewish Memory*, Philadelphia, Seattle and London, 1982. The quotation from Meyerhoff introduces chapter 4 of Yerushalmi's book, p. 79.
8. Eliezer Azikri, *Sefer Hareidim*, Jerusalem, 1958, p. 47.

Notes to Chapter Four

1. Ernest Becker, *The Denial of Death*, New York and London, 1973, p. 26.
2. *The Sacred and the Profane*, p. 25.
3. See Hayyim David Halevy, *Mekor Hayyim*, vol. 2, Jerusalem, 5743, p. 199.

Notes to Chapter Five

1. The prayers to be recited in connection with the rhythms of everyday life may be found in any Orthodox prayer book. The laws and customs relating to these rhythms are recorded in all of the codes of Jewish law. An especially good discussion in found in vol.

1 of Rabbi Hayyim David Halevy's *Mekor Hayyim*, Jerusalem, 5743.

2. *The Denial of Death*, p. 33.

Notes to Chapter Six

1. Maimonides discusses the definition of the oral law in his introduction to his commentary on the Mishnah.

2. *Mikhmanei Uziel*, Tel Aviv, 1939, p. 358.

3. *Ibid.*, p. 371.

4. *Ibid.*, p. 376.

5. *Ibid.*, p. 382.

6. *Ibid*, p. 391.

7. This material is drawn from my article, "A Sephardic Approach to Halakha," *Midstream*, August/September 1975, pp. 66-69.

8. The travel account is found in J. D. Eisenstein, *Ozar Hamasaot*, Tel Aviv, 1969. See p. 241.

9. Alan Watts, *The Supreme Identity*, New York, 1972, p. 128.

10. Andre Chouraqui, *Between East and West*, Philadelphia, 1968, p. 61.

11. H. J. Zimmels, *Ashkenazim and Sephardim*, London, 1969, p. 128f.

12. *Mikhmanei Uziel*, p. 407.

13. The text of this contract is found in Yehoshua Benveniste, *Sha'ar Yehoshua*, Husiatyn, 1904, No. 2.

14. Tam ben Yahia, *Tumat Yesharim*, Venice, 1622, No. 213, p. 112b.

15. See Schechter's essay, p. 208.

16. Isidore Epstein, *The Responsa of Rabbi Simon Duran as a Source of History of the Jews in North Africa*, New York, 1968, pp. 58-59.

17. David Ibn Zimra, *Responsa*, New York, 5727, Vol. I, 308.

18. See his commentary to *Ethics of the Fathers*, p. 103b.

19. *Ibid.*, p. 97b.

20. Appendix A to Schechter's article, p. 292.

21. Andre Chouraqui, p. 63. On the veneration of tombs of the righteous, see pp. 71f.

Notes to Chapter Seven

1. *Mikhmanei Uziel*, pp. 27f.
2. *Ibid.*, pp. 37f.
3. *Sefer Kavvanoth*, Tel Aviv, 1971, p. 59a. See also G. Scholem, *On the Kabbalah and its Symbolism*, New York, 1965, p. 65.
4. See Maimonides' discussion in his introduction to the commentary on the Mishnah.
5. See Solomon Schechter's previously cited essay on the spiritual life of Safed in the 16th century.
6. Vital's statements appear in his work, *Shaarei Kedushah*, III, 5,6,8. See R.J.Z. Werblowsky, *Joseph Karo, Lawyer and Mystic*, Philadelphia, 1977, pp. 74f.
7. See the introduction to *Maggid Mesharim*, Jerusalem, 1960.
8. Werblowsky, p. 286.

Notes to Chapter Eight

1. Judah Abrabanel, *The Philosophy of Love*, trans. F. Friedeberg-Seeley and Jean H. Barnes, London, 1937, p. 55.
2. *Ibid.*, p. 60.
3. For a discussion of techniques developed by Jewish mystics, see Aryeh Kaplan, *Meditation and Kabbalah*, New York, 1982, and *Jewish Meditation*, New York, 1985.
4. Eliezer Azikri, *Sefer Hareidim*, Jerusalem, 5718, p. 214.
5. *Ibid.*, p. 215.
6. *Sefer Gerushin*, Shklov, 5551.
7. *Ibid.*, p. 3a.
8. Mosheh Cordovero, *The Palm Tree of Deborah*, London, 1960, p. 47.
9. Judah Abrabanel, p. 49.
10. *Sefer Kavvanoth*, Tel Aviv, 1971, p. 17a.
11. Judah Abrabanel, p. 201.
12. H.Y.D. Azulai, *Abodat Hakodesh*, Warsaw, 1879, p. 6.
13. *Duties of the Heart*, treatise on humility (Sha'ar Hak'niah), chapter 8.
14. Mosheh Hayyim Luzzatto, *Mesillat Yesharim*, section on acquiring humility.
15. *The Palm Tree of Deborah*, pp. 47f.

Notes to Chapter Nine

1. *Guide for the Perplexed*, Section 3, Chapter 51.
2. See the morning service for the Ninth of Ab, *Seder Arba Taaniyoth Keminhag Sefaradim*, Vienna, 1926, pp. 182f.
3. *Mishneh Torah*, Laws of Repentance, 8:1-5. See also Maimonides' introduction to "Helek," chapter 10 of Sanhedrin.
4. Gershom Scholem, *The Messianic Idea in Judaism*, New York, 1972, p. 3.
5. *Hegyonei Uziel*, vol. 1, Jerusalem, 5713, p. 37.
6. Moshe Hayyim Luzzato, *Da'at Tevunot* (The Knowing Heart), New York, 1982.
7. Harold Kushner, *When Bad Things Happen to Good People*, New York, 1983. See especially his discussion on pp. 37f.
8. This idea is woven throughout his book, *The Lives of a Cell*, New York, 1975.
9. *Ibid.*, p. 26.
10. See the commentary of Rabbi Hayyim Ben Attar, *Or Hahayyim* on Genesis 1:17.
11. Yehudah Halevy, *The Kuzari*, New York, 1968, part 1, especially pp. 44f.

Notes to Chapter Ten

(Much of the material in this chapter was first presented at the annual meeting of The Association of Orthodox Jewish Scientists, February, 1984.)
1. Elias Canetti, *The Torch in My Ear*, New York, 1982, p. 50.
2. Ernest Becker, *The Denial of Death*, New York, 1973, p. 53.
3. Philippe Aries, *The Hour of our Death*, New York, 1981, p. 28. For a discussion of how adults deal with death, see Marc D. Angel, *The Orphaned Adult*, New York, 1986.
4. See his article, "The Concept of Death" in Robert Fulton, editor, *Death and Identity*, New York 1966, pp. 42-56.
5. Rabbi Lamm addressed a session dealing with hospice care at the General Assembly of the Council of Jewish Federations, in Atlanta, Georgia, November 17, 1983.
6. See Nahmanides' comment on Genesis 25:8.

7. See Louis Ginsburg, *Legends of the Jews*, vol. 6, Philadelphia, 1968, pp. 112-113, note 641.

8. *Legends of the Jews*, vol. 1, pp. 287-8.

9. See the responsa of Rabbi David Ibn Zimra, vol. 1, no. 256.

10. Elisabeth Kubler-Ross, *On Death and Dying*, New York, 1975.

11. *The Lives of a Cell*, pp. 58-9.

12. *Aseh Lekha Rav*, vol. 2, Tel Aviv, 5738. A lengthy discussion of the subject begins on p. 17.

Notes to Chapter Eleven

1. F. Braudel, *The Mediterranean*, vol. 2, New York, 1973, p. 826.

2. Eliyahu Benamozeg, *In Ethical Paths*, (Hebrew), Jerusalem, 1966, p. 28.

3. *Mikhmanei Uziel*, pp. 292f.

4. *Ibid.*, pp. 145f.

5. *Ibid.*, pp. 217f.

6. *Ibid.*, pp. 305.

7. The following material is drawn from my article, "A Fresh Look at Conversion," in *Midstream*, October, 1983, pp. 35-38.

8. Abraham Isaac Kook, *Da'at Cohen*, Jerusalem, 1942, p. 144, p. 155.

9. Benzion Uziel, *Mishpetei Uziel*, Jerusalem, 1964, nos. 18 and 20. See also my article, "Another Halakhic Approach to Conversions," *Tradition*, Winter/Spring 1972, pp. 107-113.

10. Yehezkel Kaufman, *Golah Venekhar*, vol. 1, Tel Aviv, 1928, pp. 226f.

11. Rabbi Shlomo Goren, responsum printed in *Shanah Beshanah*, Jerusalem, 5743, pp. 149-156.

12. Rabbi Moshe Feinstein, *Iggrot Mosheh*, 1950, Y.D. No. 160.

Notes to Chapter Twelve

1. Margaret Mead, *Culture and Commitment*, New York, 1970.

2. Emil Fackenheim, *To Mend the World*, New York, 1982, pp. 250f.

3. Rabbi Hayyim David Halevy, *Asei Lekha Rav*, vol. 1, Tel Aviv, 5736, pp. 46-48. See also vol. 2, Tel Aviv, 5738, pp. 139f.

4. Elias Canetti, *Crowds and Power*, New York, 1978, p. 178.

5. *Mikhmanei Uziel*, p. 153.

6. *Ibid.*, p. 458f.

7. Richard Rubenstein, *The Age of Triage*, Boston, 1983.

FOR FURTHER READING

Abrabanel, Judah, *The Philosophy of Love*, transl. by F. Friedeberg-Seeley and Jean H. Barnes, London, 1937.

Abudarham, David, *Abudarham Hashalem*, Jerusalem, 5723.

Angel, Marc, *The Jews of Rhodes: The History of a Sephardic Community*, New York, 1978.

———, *La America: The Sephardic Experience in the United States*, Philadelphia, 1982.

———, *The Orphaned Adult Confronting the Death of a Parent*, Jason Aronson Inc. Northvale, NJ, 1997.

———, "Ruminations on Sephardic Identity," *Midstream*, March, 1972, 64–67.

———, "Sephardic Shabbat," *Judaism*, Winter, 1982, 21–25.

Azikri, Eliezer, *Sefer Hareidim*, Jerusalem, 1958.

Benamozegh, Eliyahu, *In Ethical Paths* (Hebrew), Jerusalem, 1966.

Benattar, Hayyim, *Or Hahayyim*, commentary on the Torah, included in standard editions of the "Mikraot Gedolot."

Braudel, Fernand, *The Mediterranean*, Volume 2, New York, 1973.

Canetti, Elias, *Crowds and Power*, New York, 1978.

Chouraqui, André, *Between East and West*, Philadelphia, 1968.

Cordovero, Moshe, *The Palm Tree of Deborah*, transl. by Louis Jacobs, New York, 1974.

193

_____, *Sefer Gerushin*, Shklov, 5551.

Eliade, Mircea, *The Sacred and the Profane*, New York, 1959.

Epstein, Isidore, *The Responsa of Rabbi Simon Duran as a Source of History of the Jews in North Africa*, New York, 1968.

Ginsberg, Louis, *Legends of the Jews*, Philadelphia.

Halevy, Hayyim David, *Aseh Lekha Rav*, Volume 1, Tel Aviv, 5736.

_____, *Aseh Lekha Rav*, Volume 2, Tel Aviv, 5738.

_____, *Mekor Hayyim*, 5 volumes, Jerusalem, 5743.

Halevy, Yehudah, *The Kuzari*, transl. by H. Hirschfeld, New York, 1968.

Huli, Yaakob, *Me'am Lo'ez* on Genesis, transl. into English by Aryeh Kaplan ("Torah Anthology"), 4 volumes, New York.

Kaplan, Aryeh, *Jewish Meditation*, New York, 1985.

_____, *Meditation and Kabbalah*, New York, 1982.

Karo, Joseph, *Maggid Mesharim*, Jerusalem, 1960.

Kubler-Ross, Elisabeth, *On Death and Dying*, New York, 1975.

Luzzatto, Moshe Hayyim, *The Knowing Heart (Da'at Tevunot)*, transl. by S. Silverstein, New York, 1982.

_____, *The Path of the Just (Mesillat Yesharim)*, transl. by S. Silverstein, New York, 1980.

Maimonides, Moses, *Guide for the Perplexed*, transl. by S. Pines, Chicago, 1963.

Mead, Margaret, *Culture and Commitment*, New York, 1970.

Nahmanides, Moses, *Commentary on the Torah*, transl. by C. Chavel, 5 volumes, New York.

Papo, Eliezer, *Pele Yo-ets*, Tel Aviv.

Paquda, Bahya Ibn, *Duties of the Heart*, transl. by M. Hyamson, New York.

Schechter, Solomon, *Studies in Judaism* (second edition), Philadelphia, 1908.

Scholem, Gershom, *Major trends in Jewish Mysticism*, New York, 1967.

————, *On the Kabbalah and its Symbolism*, New York, 1965.

————, *The Messianic Idea in Judaism*, New York, 1972.

Sefer Kavanoth, Tel Aviv, 1971.

Thomas, Lewis, *The Lives of a Cell*, New York, 1975.

Uziel, Benzion, *Hegyonei Uziel*, Volume 1, Jerusalem, 5713, Volume 2, Jerusalem, 5714.

————, *Mikhmanei Uziel*, Tel Aviv, 1939.

Watts, Alan, *Nature, Man and Woman*, New York, 1970.

————, *Psychotherapy East and West*, New York, 1975.

————, *The Book*, New York, 1972.

————, *The Supreme Identity*, New York, 1972.

————, *The Wisdom of Insecurity*, New York, 1951.

Werblowsky, R.J.Z., *Joseph Karo: Lawyer and Mystic*, Philadelphia, 1977.

Yosef Hayyim of Bagdad, *Mashal Venimshal*, Jerusalem, 1913.

Yerushalmi, Yosef Hayyim, *Zakhor: Jewish History and Jewish Memory*, Philadelphia, Seattle and London, 1982.

Zeitlin, Solomon, *The Rise and Fall of the Judaean State*, 3 volumes, Philadelphia.

Zimmels, H.J., *Ashkenazim and Sephardim*, London, 1969.

INDEX

About the Author

The Rabbi of Congregation Shearith Israel, the historic Spanish and Portuguese Synagogue of New York, Marc D. Angel received his B.A., M.S., and Ph.D from Yeshiva University; rabbinic ordination from the Rabbi Isaac Elchanan Theological Seminary of Yeshiva University; and an M.A. (1970) in English Literature from the City College of New York. He was awarded an Honorary Doctor of Divinity degree from Yeshiva University in 1992. Rabbi Angel has authored and edited fourteen books, including *The Orphaned Adult: Confronting the Death of a Parent, Voices in Exile: A Study in Sephardic Intellectual History*, and a collection of essays, edited by his son, Hayyim, entitled *Seeking Good, Speaking Peace*. Rabbi Angel and his wife, Gilda, have three children: Hayyim, Ronda, and Elana.